How To

A Puppy with Love

The Essential Guide to Raising and Training a Puppy

Sarah Thompson

© **Copyright 2022 Sarah Thompson –**

All rights reserved.

The content contained within this book may not be reproduced, duplicated or transmitted without direct written permission from the author or the publisher.

Under no circumstances will any blame or legal responsibility be held against the publisher, or author, for any damages, reparation, or monetary loss due to the information contained within this book. Either directly or indirectly.

Legal Notice:

This book is copyright protected. This book is only for personal use. You cannot amend, distribute, sell, use, quote or paraphrase any part, or the content within this book, without the consent of the author or publisher.

Disclaimer Notice:

Please note the information contained within this document is for educational and entertainment purposes only. All effort has been executed to present accurate, up to date, and reliable, complete information. No warranties of any kind are declared or implied. Readers acknowledge that the author is not engaging in the rendering of legal, financial, medical or professional advice. The content within this book has been derived from various sources. Please consult a licensed professional before attempting any techniques outlined in this book.

By reading this document, the reader agrees that under no circumstances is the author responsible for any losses, direct or indirect, which are incurred as a result of the use of the information contained within this document, including, but not limited to, — errors, omissions, or inaccuracies.

Table of Contents

"Over the years I have felt the truest, purest love—the love of God, really, I imagine that's what God's love feels like—is the love that comes from your dog."

OPRAH WINFREY

Introduction

I remember like yesterday when my father brought a new puppy home. I was a little child but the memory of the excitement stays with me until the present moment, 35 years later to be exact. Even when I went by myself to choose my new puppy as an adult, the feeling was still the same.

I drove 50 miles to get my first puppy. When I arrived, a family of 6 puppies were happily playing with each other in the backyard. As they noticed me coming closer to them, they immediately turned their attention to me, humorously running towards me to get a warm, fuzzy welcome. As I saw all those beautiful creatures, I noticed that one of them had a little twisted tail in its root. Probably it unnoticeably got broken while they were playing in the backyard.

However, at the same time, she was the most adorable puppy out of all of them and I chose her to be my new best pet companion. After that, our common journey in enriching our lives began.

If you have ever owned a puppy, you know what I am talking about and if not, I am pretty sure that you will experience that in the future too, because I guess that is the reason you have bought this book and I am truly grateful for that.

As you know, everything in life has pros and cons. The excitement of a newly adopted puppy can quickly change into disappointment and frustration if not handled properly. This happens because people underestimate the amount of work and care that needs to be put in. But don't worry, it is not overly too much work, but raising a great puppy requires a good amount of work and knowledge too.

That is one of the reasons I wrote this book, to assure you that you have all it takes to be a great puppy parent, and with the knowledge I will share with you, you will be much more confident in your skills to raise a puppy with love for the benefits of both of you.

Raising a puppy is very similar to raising a baby. It is the most important stage of their life where the puppy reacts like a sponge, absorbing all the details and information we give them. Therefore it is very important to be ready for that, and act correctly so you can raise an amazing dog that will become your unconditionally loving friend.

Introduction

You will realize that raising a puppy requires patience and understanding, but rewards you with an intelligent, lovable, and loyal companion. A puppy is a fascinating, yet challenging, creature. They have an insatiable need to explore their environment, yet are easily distracted by a toy or favorite blanket. Puppies sleep a lot during the day but if they are awake, they take up the majority of your time until they are about four months old, then they become more self-sufficient, discovering the world on their own.

In this book, you will find out all the things and processes you need to know before even choosing a puppy. You will read about how to choose a puppy that will be a great match for you, and how to take perfect care of a puppy. Moreover, I will teach you more than 10 basic commands based on positive reinforcement that has worked for thousands and thousands of puppies, making a perfect pet partner for you.

As a bonus, I will teach you dog tricks that can make good fun if you ever want to brag in front of your friends or family members. You will read about stories and examples on how to treat your puppy and how it is to live with your new pet friend, some of them funny, some of them not too much but there is always a lesson to be learned.

My name is Sarah Thompson and I am an animal lover. I grew up in North Dakota helping my parents at the ranch with raising horses, milking cows, looking after hens, and of course, living with five amazing dogs. The ranch is long gone but the memories will stay with me forever. I truly love all kinds of animals because you can feel the empathy they have towards people and that made me realize how much we are connected.

You can see the change in a dog's state when you leave the house from happy to unhappy, as well as you can see how excited they get when you appear before their very eyes. Dogs have different levels of feelings regarding connection with humans, much more than any other animal. Dogs show us how much they love our presence, especially puppies.

With all that in mind, and with more than 25 years of experience in dog raising and training, I decided to share this information with you so you can also experience the joy of owning a well-behaved, happy and well-socialized dog too. I have seen hundreds, maybe thousands of puppies, studied their behavior, and helped my friends and clients to raise their puppies into amazing dogs that listen to them and make their life joyful. I want to teach you how to raise a puppy and pass on the knowledge that might be one of the best you will get regarding raising and training your puppy.

This book was written to share my experience and knowledge I have gained over the years of casual raising, as well as professional training. I have learned multiple training systems and tried many approaches. The truth is that every puppy reacts a little differently but with the information and approach described in this book, applying this knowledge can only result in a well-behaved

Introduction

dog. This book will guide you on how to raise your puppy with love, correctly, and without unnecessary punishments that can cause more damage than pleasure.

I dedicate this book to all the existing or future puppy parents that want the best for their little creatures. May positivity shine on all of you, wishing you the best of luck in your endeavors.

CHAPTER 1

How to Bond With Your Puppy

Bonding with your puppy is one of the most important things that can happen. Bonding is not only a training itself, bonding is something much deeper. There is a real energetic connection if you raise your puppy with love. You can train a dog and teach them all kinds of tricks but only through love can the puppy always find a way back to you.

Love is a state of mind. There will be times you may feel you have "fallen out of love" with your pup like the first time they nip you or when they stubbornly disobey you. Love is a commitment. Ask your puppy what love is. They know. Dogs set the standard for love. You leave them alone all day while you go to work or go play and they are heartbroken, maybe outraged. But the moment they see you, all is forgiven. They welcome you back with loving paws and a big slobbery lick on the nose. No greater love exists than the love a dog has for their human.

I have seen scared puppies, aggressive puppies, or very shy ones. It is not necessarily their genetic fault, but rather a copy of its owner. Some of those behaviors can be fixed, some of them diminished but some will never vanish, depending on the dog's personality and the impact of its owner. Therefore, there is a mindset and attributes you need to develop so you can raise and train the perfect pet partner.

Mindset and Character of a great puppy owner

Patient: Great puppy owner should be patient. There will be times your puppy won't listen perfectly. There will be times your puppy disobeys you or even does some damage. Patience is the key and knowing that these things happen and it is a part of the process makes the situation easier.

Committed: You should be committed to being the best possible parent for your puppy. In good times, and in bad times, you should be there for them.

Responsible: Having a puppy is not only fun. There are a lot of responsibilities that take place and you need to take charge of them. Vaccination, basic health care, walking, feeding, and providing daily fresh water are necessities for a puppy's healthy growth.

Accessible: Honestly, adopting a puppy just to be home alone all the time is not the best idea. You or some of your family members should always be accessible, in close surroundings to the puppy. A puppy needs to feel the presence of other people and they will bond the most with the person who will love and spend more time with them.

Trustworthy: Generally, trust isn't given; it's earned. That is not usually the case with puppies though. Unless you give them a reason not to trust you, it usually comes instilled in them. They will trust you to care for them, love, feed, water, and teach them. Don't let them down, being trusted is a privilege beyond measure.

Leader of the Pack: You've probably heard of pack order. Dogs, like wolves and many other animals, are social animals set up with a "pecking order." They have a "pack mentality" that incorporates submission and dominance. By establishing yourself, the owner and trainer, as the pack leader, your dog will naturally submit; it is in their genes to do so. Whether you are a "pack" advocate or not, there is truth to the notion, as even our children are taught to follow order by way of authority. Call it what you will, but you will need to establish your leadership with love or your puppy may very well think they are the head of the household.

How to bond with your puppy

Spending time together is everything when it comes to any relationship and the more, the better. The relationship between you and your new puppy is no exception. The warm, fuzzy feeling you get when you pet them and the moments you share looking into one another's eyes sets the scene, but it doesn't determine it.

When you first bring your puppy into your home, you will want to spend quality time together. If you can, take some days off work or school so that the two of you can bond. If that is not possible, bringing them home on your day or days off is better than during the busiest time of your week but as I said earlier, it is always better if somebody is in the puppy's presence most of the time, at least, the first month.

Keep in mind that, as mentioned earlier, your puppy has never been a puppy before. They have no idea how to act, what to do, or what to expect. It is up to you to let them know. Assure them and reassure them. When they cry at night, they are most likely missing Their mother and siblings.

Giving them love and security doesn't mean you have to bend the rules. If you have established the fact that Sweetie Pie won't be sharing your bed, gently tuck them back in when they fret, just as you would a child. If the situation gets out of hand, you may have to practice a little "tough love." Let them yelp, but do so with intervals of loving pats and kind words.

How to Bond With Your Puppy

Talking to your pup, taking them for walks, and just spending time together are priceless for setting a firm foundation, just like with human parenting. Yes, you read it right, the more you verbally talk to your puppy, the more they will catch on to things, and the closer the two of you will become. Just as you do with a baby, say the names of things like, "ball", "water" and "walk." You may be surprised how quickly they learn the names of people, places, and things. Sing to them too; dogs love a good song, though they may howl if you sing off-key.

Puppies are naturally playful, curious, and active. Those traits are going to be fun most of the time, but in order to keep your friend safe and protected, you want to help them establish boundaries. The best tip to start with is that you have to think about your puppy like you would a human child. Treat them as if they were an infant or a toddler. Here are some puppy training tips that you can use to teach your puppy everything they need to know to start the journey of becoming your best friend.

Puppy Proofing Your Home

One of the first things you will need to do with a new puppy is to puppy-proof your home. Set up gates and close doors, keeping the puppy confined to a specific space. Your little dog is probably not housebroken yet, and you don't want to clean up messes all throughout your home. Keeping the puppy within your range of sight for the first few weeks is essential. You'll also want to pick up anything that's on the ground. Puppies are famous for chewing up clothes, shoes, your child's favorite toy, and anything else they can get their eager little mouths around.

Treats and Rewards

Everyone, including puppies, loves treats. You can use these as a reward for good behavior. Dog treats come in all flavors, sizes, and specialties. Soft, meaty treats are very enticing to most puppies, and having a ready supply on hand will help your puppy quickly learn what behaviors are wanted and rewarded. Puppies usually love treats with cheese, peanut butter, or meat flavor. Select small treats instead of big ones that require a lot of chewing. The trick with training is to use quick, positive reinforcement and small, bite-sized treats as a perfect reward for your puppy but you will all learn about it later in this book.

Drop a treat into the shelter if you have one in order to lure your dog inside. Provide a treat anytime the puppy goes to the bathroom outside or sits and rolls over when commanded. Don't give your dog treats for no reason, or this will confuse the situation and they won't realize they are being rewarded. Make sure it is a suitable dog treat that you're providing as well.

Your rewards should also vary. If you always give them a treat following a voice command, they will associate the command with food. If they don't want or need food, then he'll refuse the command. Instead, if your reward includes giving them a treat, soothing them, playing with them, or petting them, then they know that they will get some type of reward when following the command. This way a puppy will learn to always listen to your commands not only expecting some type of treat. Anything that produces positive feelings such as playing or petting them counts.

Communicating Your Intentions Clearly

There's nothing wrong with explicitly telling your puppy "no", only that it often fails to offer enough information. Instead, you can tell them what you want. Dogs don't usually generalize well, so if the dog jumps on someone in excitement and you say "no", they may jump higher or change direction. A better alternative would be to instruct them to sit. Telling them what you want helps avoid confusion.

One of the biggest mistakes when trying to use voice commands is using too many words. Your dog can associate words, but it takes some time. You'll want a word that is to the point. Finish learning one command before moving on to another. If you move on to other commands too quickly, then your dog may get confused.

Be Consistent

You have to be consistent if you want your puppy to be consistent. You can't work for an hour on a sit command and then just not take up their training again for a week or two. You have to work on the same command daily until they get it right.

Establish routines with your puppy, such as regular feeding times, walk, and play times, and bathroom breaks. Stick with your routines and this will help speed up the process. It's not just about training commands either. A routine for your puppy will help them get up when you do, play when you feel up to it, and eat when you are able to feed them. This way you aren't rearranging your schedule to take care of your puppy. Instead, you'll be teaching them to work on your schedule so that they work with you.

If you don't want your puppy to jump on people when they come through the front door, you need to reinforce that expectation every time. Allowing the pup to jump all over your sister, but not your neighbor will cause confusion. Use the "sit" or "stay" or "heel" command (you will learn later in this book) to get your puppy's attention and do it every time. Be consistent since inconsistencies will only confuse them and prolong the training process.

Use Repetition

Repetition is key in dog training. Dogs learn from repetition. The certain command will become linked with certain behavior in the puppy's brain. It needs to be done with precision and good timing. If the puppy performs your command, reward it immediately. If not, ignore it and try again until it is done successfully.

Be Patient

Even more patience, but YES, it is a crucial quality. Don't allow yourself to get frustrated or impatient during the training process – either with yourself or with your new puppy. It will take some time to accomplish all the goals you have set for your new pal and for you to get the hang of your puppy's unique personality, likes, and the techniques and rewards that work best for your puppy.

Give your puppy time to understand new commands. They most likely won't learn it the first couple of times when you teach them. Repeat old commands in new training sessions, so that they don't forget them. The attention span of a dog is pretty short, so keep your sessions frequent but short in duration, otherwise, your pup will become bored.

Never get impatient with your puppy and never call them to you if you are going to punish them – all that will do is teach them that coming to you is not a good thing. The only way you do it when you spot unwanted behavior is to come to the puppy, call them their name to get their attention, and give a new command, if done successfully, reward immediately saying "Good boy/girl". Keep your voice firm but gentle, and never let any frustration creep into it.

Train Yourself

When you introduce a new dog into your household and your life, you're not just training the puppy. You're training yourself as well. Your life is going to have to change, and you need to be prepared for it and willing to adapt. Sleeping in until noon on the weekends is no longer an option when you have a puppy that needs to be walked and fed. Taking off for a spontaneous vacation sounds like fun, but first, you'll have to make arrangements for the pup. Working with the dog to be calm and quiet when friends and family visit takes a lot of energy and a willingness to hang in there for the long term.

Possible causes of not bonding with your puppy

Possible causes of not bonding with your puppy are the opposite of what you should do to properly bond with your puppy. Not being available, being impatient, and punishing the puppy in the wrong way and wrong time.

One of my clients, Trisha, had multiple problems with her new puppy. She adopted a male Staffordshire terrier and called him Tyson. On our first appointment, she told me she adopted this breed purely because she just loved it. She didn't do any research beforehand, she got advice from her friends who had a dog on how to train him.

Because Trisha was a young, busy woman living on her own, spending a lot of time at work, she wasn't available for the puppy as she should be. Anytime she got back home, there were excrements all over the place because she didn't want to lock the puppy in a crate. The problem was that she punished that puppy for the excrement by pulling their fur a bit.

Sometimes when she got back home, her clothes were chewed-up in pieces because the puppy got bored. Of course, the puppy was punished for that too. When Trisha was practicing obedience training with Tyson, after multiple times of commanding the word "Sit" and failing to do so, she bent over and hugged him saying "You are my little devil, aren't you?" and kissed him.

I knew right away what was wrong. We started fixing all those things right away. First, because there couldn't be any other person involved, we only had one option. Train her puppy to stay only in one room.

Trisha decided to clean up one of her rooms and install a pet gate, leaving nothing else besides food, water, and lots of chewing toys for her little devil. Because a puppy needs to be walked more often than an adult dog, her brother could stop by and take Tyson for a walk. That didn't stop Tyson from having a little accident every now and then but more human contact between Tyson and Trisha's brother was created and that is always useful.

Since then, Tyson wasn't punished anymore because that simply didn't make sense. Firstly, the puppy can't link the punishment with the accident that took place an hour ago. Now you are punishing a puppy and they don't know the reason behind the punishment. Secondly, as you know and you will read in this book, we are raising a puppy with love. We don't punish our puppies. We notify them and then correct them by commanding desired behavior, but definitely not physically punishing them.

Lastly, if your dog doesn't repeatedly listen to your commands, you don't pet him saying "You are my little devil, aren't you? Why? Because that reinforces the puppy's disobedience. If the puppy repeatedly doesn't listen, you either ignore it or let it go completely. Maybe the puppy might be tired at the moment, distracted by something else, or you don't communicate clearly to them. Either way, there is a neutral reaction and you move on and try later.

Since then, Trisha and Tyson have developed a much better, healthier, and more understanding relationship. If you have the right information, things go much easier. There are hundreds of situations and relationships that don't go well. If that happens, we should never blame the puppy, but look at ourselves first. We are responsible for the development of our puppy; the personality and behavior the puppy will possess in the future is merely from our contribution.

So now you have a great notion of how to connect with your new puppy. You have found out what mindset it takes to be a great puppy parent and you know how the puppy feels about being in a new home with new people. You also know what are the causes of not bonding with your puppy and how to prevent that before it happens. In the next chapter, we will discuss how to choose the right breed for you, and I will break down particular dog breeds so you can be more confident in choosing the right match for you. Let's get to it.

CHAPTER 2

Choosing the Right Breed of Puppy

Y ou've made the decision to move forward and bring a new puppy into your life and home. It's exciting and joyful, and it can be difficult to be patient when you're so ready to bring that new little bundle of joy home.

BUT, rushing out to the local pet store, or checking out the classifieds and dashing off to buy the first little pup that chews on your shoelaces can be a bad idea for so many reasons!

There are over 340 recognized dog breeds that fall into one of six categories - toy, sporting, hound, terrier, working, and herding.

However, it's very important to remember that each breed has its own very specific 'look', personality and needs, and so do you and your family members. Let's have a look at the top 12 Family dog breeds so you can get a sense of similarities or differences in particular dogs.

Top 12 Family Dog Breeds

1. Labrador Retriever

Labrador Retriever is one of my favorites! Highly intelligent, good-natured, very willing, and eager to please. These lively dogs have an excellent, reliable temperament and are friendly, superb with children, and equable with other dogs. They can perform all kinds of tricks.

2. Golden Retriever

These are lovable, well-mannered, intelligent dogs with great charm. They are easily trained, always patient, and gentle with children. Fantastic family member.

3. Beagle

The Beagle is loving, sweet, and gentle, happy to see everyone, greeting them with a wagging tail. It is sociable, brave, and intelligent.

4. German Shepherd

German Shepherd dogs are extremely faithful, and brave. They will not think twice about giving their lives for their human pack. They have a high learning ability. German Shepherds love to be close to their families, but can be wary of strangers. This breed needs its people and should not be left isolated for long periods of time.

5. Boxer

The Boxer is happy, high-spirited, playful, curious, and energetic. Highly intelligent, eager, and quick to learn, the Boxer is a good dog for competitive obedience. It is constantly on the move and bonds very closely with the family. Loyal and affectionate, Boxers are known for the way they get along so well with children.

6. Bulldog

The Bulldog is among the gentlest of dogs. Just the same it will see off any intruder. It is described as a very affectionate and dependable animal, gentle with children, but known for its courage and its excellent guarding abilities. Bulldogs are very much a people's dog, seeking out human attention and loving every bit they can get!! A lot of human attention is required for the breed's happiness.

7. Dachshund

You might know this dog as a "sausage dog". Long body, short legs, you know. Some might have a funny look but, Dachshunds are great travelers. This little dog needs an owner who understands how to be their pack leader or they will take over the house, and begin to try and tell the owner what to do.

8. Pitbull

Pitbulls are very loyal, beautiful dogs. They are also quite protective of their home and what they view as their territory. This can make them a bit possessive and aggressive. A Pitbull needs stability, firmness, and consistent training in order to be well-behaved in the home. These dogs are very athletic and need a lot of movement and activities.

9. Staffordshire terrier

The Staffordshire Terrier is an intelligent, courageous, and determined dog, which makes them great watchdogs. This breed is not for everyone, however. Very similar to Pitbull, Staffordshire Terrier is an athletic breed that needs to be loaded with activities.

10. Goldendoodle

A Goldendoodle is a friendly, energetic dog that loves to play and be engaged. They love attention and will thrive in an active family. A Goldendoodle makes a great family pet. Very lovely and passionate breed.

11. Jack Russell Terrier

Jack Russell Terrier loves to play and loves people. This breed is good with children and other dogs, but may not do well with cats. They are clever, fun-loving, and affectionate.

12. Border Collie

Border Collie is an intelligent, active, and eager-to-please dog. This breed is highly trainable and makes a great companion for any type of family. Border Collies are energetic, outgoing, and very friendly dogs. They will do well with children in the right situation. They need regular exercise or they will start to get themselves into trouble! They can also perform an incredible amount of tricks, and they are learning very quickly.

Dogs vary in many aspects, not just in character. Size, height, and weight play a major role in adulthood. Therefore it is very important to be clear of what you want to deal with; because as a puppy, any breed is manageable because of its size, but as the puppy grows, there will be situations that you will need to cope with.

Before you choose your new puppy, it is crucial to mirror your own life too. Sometimes we would like a particular breed but that would not go well with our lifestyle or way of living, possibly causing more problems than pleasures. It is good to know what to look for when choosing a puppy and here are 10 important considerations from the owner's perspective when choosing a puppy.

8 Important Considerations When Choosing A New Puppy

Do you have children?

If so, then you'll want to choose a breed that has the right temperament for kids. Your kids will also have to be dog-friendly — prepare for the extra steps it takes to teach them to train the dog, and to respect their space.

The majority of dogs will get along with children just fine if they are raised with them. However, some breeds have a protective streak in them and may become aggressive with children who get too close at mealtime, or aggressive with children they've never met.

These breeds will likely see the children as being underneath themselves in the "pack order" and may try to dominate them.

Some dogs will patiently put up with little children who pull their ears or accidentally poke them in the eyes, while others will not and may nip or bite back in defense.

So if you want a dog who is excellent with children avoid breeds that may have a dominance streak or that have short tempers.

Do You Already Have Other Dogs In Your Home?

Remember, all dogs, even domesticated ones, have a pack mentality. Bringing a new puppy into "your pack" involves additional steps. Watch your prospective puppy at the shelter to see how they get along with the other dogs. If the puppy is combative there, it's a very strong indicator that it would be combative at your home as well.

Puppies with Coats and Shedding

Dogs with long coats require daily brushing or else their coats will become matted and tangled. Not only can it hurt your dog if they have tangled and matted hair, but it will also become dirty and they will look shaggy and ugly if you don't regularly brush their coat.

So keep in mind that if you choose a breed with a long coat you will either need to get it clipped regularly if you want to avoid brushing it so much, or if you choose to keep it long or even medium length you will have to brush it every day.

Does Your Work Require A Lot Of Travel?

Do you have to travel for work or have a long commute? If so, do you have assistance or are you able to invest in help while you're away?

What Type of Lifestyle Do You Have – Active or Sedentary?

You need to be honest with yourself, because each type of dog has its own needs and level of care. Are you sure you're willing to take your dog walking for 30-minutes on a cold February morning? If you are not too much for a long, active walk then consider a breed that is not too demanding. Adopting a Pitbull or Jack Russell Terrier might not be the best match for you.

Do You Live in a Home With a Yard or a Small Condo or Apartment?

That cute little puppy you have your eye on may be small now, but will it grow into a large, active dog? If so, maybe you should rethink your dream breed. Remember, though, that even some smaller, more active dogs can take up a lot of space (and energy) in their own way.

Can You Afford the puppy?

Bringing a new puppy into your life and home requires a commitment just like the commitment to be responsible for a child. This is a commitment that shouldn't be taken lightly.

It can vary by breed, but your puppy could end up costing you from $600 to roughly $900 each year — beyond what you paid for accessories and to adopt them. So, before you commit, make a budget and figure out what you can handle. Also remember, a puppy won't be a puppy forever. As they grow, they will eat more and hopefully will always be healthy so you will never have to worry about expensive veterinary bills.

Recurring veterinary bills?

There are initial costs that can include the following - $200 to spay or neuter — plus $150 for the first exam, another $150 for vaccinations, $130 for heartworm testing. It's smart to plan how you'll pay for ongoing medical care. Put aside an extra $210 for toy breeds and up to $260 for a large dog, and definitely consider pet health insurance. (The price can vary state to state, also that is the cost of time writing this book)

Where To Find Your New Puppy

Essentially, you have three options – You can go to a shelter, contact a rescue group, or go to a breeder.

Fortunately, the internet is an integral part of everyday life and society. There are now online sites that can help you locate puppies that are up for adoption.

Almost every county and the bigger city has a shelter run by the local government, as well as others run by nonprofit groups. Some will have state-of-the-art facilities, and others may be more basic but, as a rule, dogs from shelters will have had shots and possibly some basic training because these make them more adoptable.

Don't be misled into thinking that shelters only have mutts and mixed breeds. It is estimated that 25 percent of dogs up for adoption are purebreds who have been given up for many reasons.

Adopting From a Shelter

Before you go to a shelter, you want to prepare yourself emotionally because it's easy to get caught up and swept away by all those cute, pleading faces.

Here's What You Need To Know Before You Go

If possible, try to pick a shelter that is close to your home so you can easily make several visits if you're having difficulty choosing a puppy.

Ideally, you want to get a real sense of a puppy's personality. It's a good idea to ignore a puppy at first, but stand or sit nearby, so they can get used to your presence and your scent.

If you face the dog or try to talk to them, they have to adjust to you, and you won't be able to get to really know them.

Body language and energy are very important and you'll want to pay close attention to them. Ears perked up and tail held high? That may signal an excited, dominant state, which you shouldn't reward with attention. Give attention to a submissive dog whose head is slightly down and whose tail is wagging but held halfway up.

Dogs that rush to the front of the cage are showing signs of anxiety, frustration, or dominance. A puppy that cowers at the back of the cage may have shyness issues that can translate into fear-related aggressiveness.

Try to narrow your choice down to two or three. Take each one for a short leash walk and ask the shelter workers about the puppy's personalities and habits. Do they have any health issues, for example? Or have they been adopted and returned? If so, why? Prepare your list of questions and get down to a business.

Choosing a Good Breeder

As with trying to choose any service provider, getting referrals is a great resource. If people speak well of a breeder, then that's a great sign that they take care of their animals and have high standards. Some great places to get referrals are vets, the American Kennel Club (AKC), and local breed clubs.

A good breeder will be able to answer questions about the dog's ancestry (remember to ask about parents' and grandparents' temperaments. This will tell you a great deal).

The energy level is critical, so be sure to ask about it. Pay attention to behavior. If a pup bounces off the walls at the breeder's, he'll probably do it at your home.

It's a great idea to ask the breeder for the contact information of other people who have adopted puppies from them. Make sure you see several puppies, so you can find the one you're most comfortable — and compatible — with.

This is really important – No good breeder will ever let you adopt a puppy that's younger than eight weeks old. A reputable breeder always has the best interest of the puppy and the new prospective owner. When choosing a puppy from a shelter, breeder, or rescue group, always rely on great reviews and references.

Your puppy can be formed in any set of behavior you would please but that won't apply 100% of the time. There are natural instincts and inherited traits that make your puppy unique. If you want to know who your puppy is in the depth, optionally you can perform a set of these tests.

Puppy Personality Testing

There is no "one size fits all" and personality and temperament aren't cast in stone at birth.

However, the concept of "puppy testing" by giving a puppy a few simple tests has gained popularity throughout the dog world. One of the best-known series of tests is the "Volhard Test", which is named after the couple who standardized their own testing techniques to help identify a dog's personality.

The practical reason behind such a test is to gauge a puppy's "dominance level", or how headstrong they are by nature. An extremely bold dog is going to be a handful to train, while at the other end of the spectrum the very shy puppy—who can be startled by its own shadow— will be difficult to train for different reasons.

Puppy personality testing also gives a sense of a puppy's level of interest in people, which has a direct effect on their trainability and how easily he'll become a member of "your pack".

Age for Testing

Seven weeks—forty-nine days to be exact—is considered to be the ideal age for a puppy to be evaluated away from the litter. Except for a small amount of learned behavior, a seven-week-old puppy is thought to be a clean slate, meaning that testing at this time is supposed to give a true reading of their nature.

Puppy-Testing Situations

Of course, there are variations on how puppies may respond to any of these "pop tests," but I include only two ends of the spectrum: anything in between is your judgment call. But in the case of very dominant or very submissive dogs, you can predict that they will behave almost the same way in every situation.

It's up to you whether you try some or all of these experiments, but try not to get too serious about them. Just use them as a baseline test to get a general idea of the puppy's temperament.

The prevailing wisdom is that you should avoid any personality extremes in a pup: not the laid-back puppy, but not the most forward and pushy one, either. Other than that, try some of the little tests that follow—"Pop Tests for Pups," you might call them—and see which appeals to you as a way to get to know a puppy quickly.

Puppy Testing Guidelines

- Use a room that is unfamiliar to the pups.
- Perform the tests when the puppies are at their most active.
- Puppies get a confidence boost from their litter mates, so perform the test individually.

Personality Test #1 - Shows whether a dog accepts social domination

Bend down and firmly stroke from the puppy's head down to the top of their shoulders. A dog's head, neck, and shoulders are dominant areas: when two dogs meet, the higher-ranking one will often put their paw or chin across the withers (the ridge between the shoulder bones) of the other.

Ideally, a puppy will probably not object to this. They might whine, wiggle, or stiffen for a moment, but then he'll relax and even lick you.

A dominant puppy will likely object to your dominating stroking of them—they may growl or try to jump on you. They may panic, struggle or freeze and not snap out of it.

Personality Test #2 - This test measures curiosity and eagerness about people. Do they enjoy human affection enough to work for it in training?

Bend down, clap your hands, but don't call the puppy right away—just watch. Ideally, a puppy comes right over, and will stay with you, wagging its tail. A dominant puppy may bite at you or wander away disinterested.

Personality Test #3 - Call the Puppy to You: crouch down, clap your hands, whistle, sound encouraging

Bend down, and open your arms for the most welcoming position. A dominant puppy might ignore you, or come straight at you and nip, jump or bump into you when they get there.

Personality Test #4 - Will They Follow You?

Stroke the puppy, walk away, then see how readily they follow. Ideally, a puppy follows you.

A dominant puppy follows, but so close that they get underfoot and might even try to bite at your feet or clothes.

Personality Test #5- Hold the Puppy Off the Floor: Cradle Your Hands Under Their Stomach

What does the puppy do when they have no control and you have total control?

Gently lift them a few inches off the ground and hold the position for fifteen seconds.

Ideally, a puppy struggles a little, then relaxes in your hands.

A dominant puppy will struggle and fight and may bark, whine or try to bite your hands.

Personality Test #6: Sit down and hold the puppy on their back in your lap: stroke their belly, speak reassuringly

What is their reaction to being gently restrained?

Ideally, a puppy will struggle briefly and then relax.

A dominant puppy will thrash around to get off its back and may vocalize or bite.

Personality Test #7: -Retrieving. Set the puppy on the floor, get their attention by waving a ball or toy, and then roll it across the floor. Make enthusiastic, encouraging, "Come on girl/boy!" noises to bring it back.

Ideally, a puppy will chase the object, play with it and maybe even bring it back to you if you clap your hands and whistle. They will let you take it away without too much objection.

A dominant puppy will chase the object and take off with it, ignoring you when you try to recall them. If you try to take it back they won't relinquish it and may growl.

So there you go. You have already learned something, haven't you? In this chapter you have learned about different tempers shown by dogs, you found out what to consider when choosing a puppy to be the right match and you have learned how to test a puppy for its level of dominance which can be useful in your training endeavors. You also know where to go to choose your puppy, and what to search for. You are all set to make things happen, now things start to get exciting because in the next chapter you are about to find out the best way to transition your puppy from litter to your new home, how your first day together should look like, and much more. Are you ready? So turn the page.

CHAPTER 3

Easy Transitioning of a Puppy from Litter to New Home

Puppies are tiny, defenseless, and far away from their mother, so they need extra care and a watchful eye to ensure that they grow healthfully. You might be a bit overwhelmed and confused as to how exactly you should go about doing so, and it's only natural that you feel this way. With some research and careful planning, though, you'll surely become a skillful fur-parent in no time.

Bringing a new puppy home is a delightful treat for the whole family, one that can significantly brighten everyone's day. Since granting a safe and loving home for a puppy is no small feat, there are a few things to consider ahead of time. You want to bring your puppy into a puppy-ready environment. Here is a list of things you might consider buying.

Prepare Essentials For Your Puppy

Dog-proof fence

Canines are naturally curious creatures. The good news is, if they ever find their way out, they'll likely be able to follow the scent back home. However, there's plenty to worry about beyond the fence of your home that could seriously injure your dog, and in some extreme cases, result in its death.

If you don't have a fence right now, don't bring your dog home in the hope of keeping it as a strictly indoor pet. Even if you walk your dog every morning, you're still going to want it to wander about in your yard for some moderate sun exposure, and to give it extra space to explore and get enough exercise without having to be on a leash.

Dogs also tend to get bored easily, so access to the backyard will allow them to watch your neighbors and maybe even chase some squirrels. Don't worry, it's unlikely that they'll catch any of them.

Another reason you want to get a fence is that it allows your best friend to freely get frequent bathroom breaks. This is especially important when it's still a puppy; you'll have to teach it where it's okay to go potty, or else you'll have a lot to clean up on a daily basis.

Just remember that getting a fence does not replace taking your dog on a walk. Dogs need to be walked every day for a change of scenery, an adequate amount of exercise, and some mental stimulation. This also helps you bond with your new puppy and gives it something to look forward to every day.

Pet gates

When you're adopting a young pup, you're going to have to keep the nosy little furball away from parts of your home that could be dangerous for it to explore, or any other place that you'd like to keep clean and tidy. Canines are curious and messy, and any room they access may end up being subject to a few chewed-up objects or broken vases.

There are gates specifically designed for pets, but some are so low that your puppy can learn to leap over them. Make sure the gates you go for are both high and sturdy enough.

I recommend you get these installed at multiple entrances; although, you shouldn't keep them closed at all times. They can be a great way to discipline your dog not to interrupt you while you're cooking or eating. For the first few months, expect your dog to bark and wail at the closed gate. It will be heartbreaking, but eventually, your dog will learn when and where it can access areas in your home.

The possibilities are endless when it comes to where you can install pet gates, but I would advise against overusing them. Dogs expect to be treated as part of the family. If you restrict their access to multiple areas for prolonged periods of time, this also limits the time you spend with your dog, which can take a toll on their mental health. Use the gates in moderation, when you absolutely have to.

Chew toys

Think of chewing toys as pacifiers for babies. In their teething phase, puppies will either chew on the numerous toys that you provide them, or they'll chew holes through your furniture. There's no third option.

Chewing for growing puppies is akin to an itch that needs to be scratched, and it helps them grow healthy teeth quickly. However, that's not to say that fully-grown dogs will stop using their chew toys. Wild canines naturally exert a lot of effort while chewing through the flesh and bones of their prey—a natural instinct that canned or dry food does not satiate. Because your dog doesn't go out to hunt, it needs to find something else to chew on other than prey.

Your options are endless, and your preferences fully depend on your dog. Most canines, especially puppies, enjoy squeaky toys because they mimic squealing prey. It may sound gruesome, but it's only instinct. You'll most likely want to provide your puppy with a variety of toys to choose from.

Bigger plush toys will be their favorite to occasionally chew on, and also use as snuggle pillows when they nap. Bone-shaped squeaky toys are usually great distractions to pass the time, or to enjoy some quality playtime with you.

If you'll leave your dog unaccompanied for a few hours, the best toy to keep it entertained with is a rubber chew treat toy, which can be filled with treats that ooze out of the toy when bit or squeezed. This also mimics a hunting experience, which will keep your dog's instincts satiated, and will, in turn, help keep your pet well-behaved.

There are also flavored toys, which double as toothbrushes for your pup. These toys are specially designed with soft bristles that clean your dog's teeth as it chews on the toy. They're great for some extra dental care, but don't forget that they can't replace a thorough tooth brushing routine. Some canines are also finicky when it comes to cheap rubber that smells artificial. Opt for a flavored toy to make it more appealing to your dog.

Food and water accessories

You should invest in some sturdy and easy-to-clean food and water bowls as soon as you can. Growing puppies have enormous appetites and you need to make sure that you have the right tools on hand to feed them regularly. It's advisable to get a fairly large water bowl, too, as all dogs need easy access to clean, fresh water at all times.

Furthermore, you should put your puppy on a diet recommended by the vet as they might want to modify their meal plans according to any specific concerns or ailments currently aggravating your puppy.

An automatic food dispenser will be your best friend (aside from your furry companion) if you spend long hours at work every day. Even if you feed your dog as soon as you get back home, it's best to schedule timed feedings for your pet, especially since dogs truly thrive on routine.

Many dog feeders can be timed to regulate your pet's eating schedule, and you get to choose how much you want to feed on a daily basis, as well. This will also help if your dog tends to wake you up early in the morning, demanding to be fed.

Feeders can work with wet or dry food depending on the model, and different brands cater to different sizes.

Timed 12-meal automatic feeders are considered the best and healthiest option for small or medium-sized dogs. This way, instead of eating two big meals, they're fed 12 smaller meals throughout the day. The slow feed mode slowly dispenses food over the course of 15 minutes to prevent your dog from vomiting, which usually happens when dogs eat too quickly.

But that doesn't mean that the machine gets to pick when and how your dog eats. If you want to set an eating schedule for your dog on your own terms for medical reasons, there's an immediate feed mode that allows you to select the portion of food served as well.

Whatever dispenser you choose for your dog, make sure you take out the tray or bowl to clean it every day.

Dog house

Dog house becomes more relevant when your puppy turns ideally 6 months old. If you have a house with a backyard and plan to keep your dog freely outside, consider building a dog house. Dogs should always be allowed to come inside whenever they want to, but if they regularly spend time in your backyard (and they probably will), it's best to build a comfortable dog house for them.

For starters, this creates a space for them that they feel is their own. Just like your household members have a room of their own, a dog house will be your pet's personal space. Dog houses can also protect your pets from heat strokes; however, if it's even moderately hot for you outside, it's likely too hot for your dog. Make sure that whatever dog door you have installed can be locked when necessary, so you can keep your buddy indoors when the weather conditions are not ideal.

You don't have to spend hundreds of dollars on custom-made dog houses that match the exterior design of your home. Any generic den made of white cedar will be quite durable, and also safe for your dog. White cedar is also known as stained white wood, and the reason why it makes the perfect material for dog houses is that it's naturally non-toxic for pets and gives off a pleasing scent even when wet.

Aside from being an aesthetically pleasing addition to your yard, it's also resistant to severe weather changes as well as pests that may infest your garden, so you can rest assured that your dog will be safe under its little sloped roof.

If you're going to make your purchase online, make sure you select the correct size. Dogs, in general, enjoy cozy spaces, so anything too commodious for your fur baby is not recommended. Whatever you pick, I recommend you get one with floor panels, so your dog doesn't have to take a nap on a wet lawn.

Grooming kit

You should at least have a basic grooming kit at home, even if you plan to regularly take your dog to a professional groomer.

Grooming isn't just about keeping your dog looking adorable. Trimming a dog's fur and nails regularly is sanitary and helps you spot any signs of potential infections or illnesses. Grooming your pet regularly will also minimize coat and skin issues like consistent scratching, rashes, bumps, and matting. Combing your dog's hair evenly distributes hair oils, which means your dog will have a healthier and shinier coat.

Your kit should usually have a comb, scissors, trimmers, and clippers. Depending on the breed, many dogs will be particularly scared of loud clippers. There are many silent ones on the market specifically created for timid puppies. If you're unsure if your dog will take grooming well, go for the silent kit, and remember that its perception of this experience can always be improved with lots of love, praise, and treats.

Before grooming, make sure your dog is bathed. If your dog regularly plays outside, a weekly bath should suffice. Do not bathe your dog more than once weekly.

If your puppy has a thick coat, untangle any knots before you bathe it. Use lukewarm water and diluted dog shampoo. Never use soap or human shampoo on dogs, although some people may choose to use horse shampoo for thicker and shinier coats.

With certain breeds, you'll want to invest in a stripping knife. Dogs that do not naturally shed hair will need you to manually strip overgrown and dead hair. Make sure your dog is comfortable with being stripped, or else this process will be extremely inconvenient for both you and your pet.

Use nail clippers to keep your dog's nails trimmed. If you don't cut them regularly, they'll be more difficult to cut the next time you try to do it. Standard scissors work fine, but I recommend the guillotine clipper. If you skip this step, it will become increasingly difficult for your dog to walk, as their nails will grow into a curve that pricks at their paws as they move around.

Aside from trimming nails and hair, make sure you regularly comb your dog to remove any shed hair and keep its coat clean and tangle-free.

Collar or Harness and leash

Although they may be the most obvious ones on the list, they're definitely essential items regardless of where you're keeping your puppy until it grows up. Walking your puppy can help the two of you bond, and will make it grow to be more comfortable around humans. and socialize with other dogs.

When it comes to collars, ID tags are essential to make sure that your pet will always be identified in case it loses its way. Puppies are generally hyperactive and fun-loving, so make sure that your leash is a good fit; otherwise, you may suddenly lose your grip if your puppy sees a familiar neighbor in the distance, or a stray animal it wants to chase.

Optionally, you can get your puppy microchipped, which will allow you to find out exactly where it is. If a microchipped dog ever gets lost and someone takes it to a vet, they will use your information to contact you and bring your dog back.

When picking collars, make sure it's the right fit. Collars that are too tight can be extremely uncomfortable for your dog, while others may slip off easily. Whatever you choose, make sure that you have extras laying around so you can easily replace them if they get lost.

From my personal experience, I prefer a harness over a collar. This is because, with a harness, I feel like I have better control over the dog. Also, if the dog suddenly pulls, I won't start choking them with a collar, instead, I will pull them back to its body, using a harness. Harness works perfectly for all dog sizes; so you don't have to worry if that would be suitable for yours. Either way, the final decision is up to you.

Carrier

Carriers for bigger dogs are tricky business, but it's nothing that your local pet shop cannot guide you through. Your puppy will likely fit in any plastic carrier, but as your dog grows up, you'll find yourself switching between bigger sizes.

You should always know the weight and measurements of your dog before you head to a pet shop. Measure your dog from the base of its neck to the root of its tail, then add a few inches for the head and tail. The height should also be calculated, and the weight of your dog contributes to the material you'll opt for to make sure it's sturdy enough for your dog's size.

There are plastic and wooden carriers, as well as soft-sided ones. It all depends on how you plan to use them. If you're on your way to a flight, soft-sided carriers can easily be placed under seats. But if your dog is traveling in cargo, make sure the carrier is hard, sturdy, and most importantly, well-ventilated.

If you're using your carrier for vet trips, backpack carriers work great for smaller puppies. Bigger dogs can easily be carried to a car or taken on public transportation.

Whatever carrier you buy, make sure it is durable. If you cheap out on your pet shopping spree, you might end up repurchasing everything. Bear in mind that dogs can easily escape cheap fabric carriers.

Dog bed

It doesn't matter if you plan to have your dog sleep next to you; your pet should always have a bed of its own. Just like dog houses, dog beds are part of your best friend's personal bubble. And the fact is, dogs will likely choose their own beds over yours.

There are plenty of dog beds out there, and each depends on the sleeping style of your dog. You can get a sprawler, a burrower, a curler, or a leaner. Shape and design aside, you need to make sure that you purchase the correct size, which isn't too spacious or too small for your dog but most importantly, buy a comfortable one.

You'll find different fabrics on the market. Most of them don't make a difference, as long as you check the label or description of the product and make sure that it's machine-washable, bearing in mind that dog beds will need to be washed regularly.

Piddle pads and newspapers

Unfortunately, some dogs can be harder to train, and the first few weeks at your home will probably be a bit of an adventure. Adding to that is the fact that puppies tend to leak, so you'll need to keep your home stocked with all sorts of training pads and line the floors with newspapers until your pet gets the lay of the land.

When Bella, my now 11-year-old Labrador Retriever, was a 9 weeks old puppy, I had her sleeping right next to my bed. She had a beautiful puppy bed and because she felt my presence, she didn't even cry from missing her mummy. I woke up one night with an urge to go to the bathroom, and I always go in the dark without switching the light on because I knew my apartment.

Well, don't do that if you have a new puppy in the room. Bella pooped all over the place and as I walked I stepped right into one of those unpleasant surprises. Instead of going back to sleep, I had to wash and clean my apartment while Bella was happily sleeping.

A veterinarian

While that's not something you can get at the store, it's something you need to be prepared for before you adopt a new puppy.

Some people tend to think of vet centers as places your pet only needs to visit when it's ill. Not true, especially in a puppy's early months. That said, your dog will have to be regularly dewormed and will eventually have to be neutered or spayed, if this hasn't already been done by the shelter or breeder. Ask the rescuer/breeder of your puppy if it has already been vaccinated so your vet knows what they are dealing with.

Don't just pick the closest vet to your home. Make sure you check reviews before you decide to trust a vet with your puppy. If taking your dog to the vet is too much of a hassle, home visits are also an option, but can be fairly more expensive.

Even though getting a dog might sound like a heartwarming idea, it's also a huge responsibility. So, before you make the big decision, make sure that your work schedule allows you to invest in bringing up a puppy. And if this is the first pet you own, be sure to contact your local vet before you bring your dog home, to be made aware of the check-ups you'll have to make to keep your dog happy and healthy.

Your First Trip

Your first trip with your puppy will be the one from the place you take the puppy from. It is a good idea to be prepared for that journey but that, of course, depends on how far you go and which transport you get. If it is a long distance(driving more than 1 hour) and travel by car, preferably take one more person with you. This journey might be stressful for your new puppy. It is always better if the puppy is held by somebody else and also for safety reasons.

If you have no option to take another person with you, then it is advisable you use a carrier or any bigger box; that will also do the job. If you are able to use a seat belt over it for the safety of the puppy, that would be wonderful. Depending on the distance, take some water, bowl, collar, or harness and treats with you. You might stop in the middle of the way and walk your puppy a bit. If your trip won't take longer than 1 hour, you practically don't need anything as your puppy should be well fed and emptied to last an hour.

What Should The First Day In A New Home Look Like

So you chose your new puppy and safely transferred it to your home. What is next?

First of all, the first day with a new puppy should be slow and full of fun. The dog will likely miss its mother or siblings, so you have to show them that you're there for them. And what's better for puppies than playing?

During the first day, your puppy is going to be overly excited about everything in its surroundings. To make sure your puppy doesn't get overwhelmed and exhausted by all the excitement, keep its paws on the ground. You can start by giving it a bed and rewarding it when it uses its bed.

Trust is an important part of a new relationship, and you're going to have to earn it. Let your dog explore at its own pace and slowly introduce it to your family, or just leave it alone in a room and wait for the puppy to come out on its own. Take care not to scare your puppy with any quick movements.

As far as food goes, make sure you feed your dog often and don't overfeed it. You can also mix dog food with milk or water. If your dog doesn't finish its meal, don't worry, as it's normal for a young puppy to play with its food instead of actually eating it. You can also opt for wet food, as long as it's not canned.

Tips And Tricks To Avoid Puppy's Homesickness

If you've ever experienced homesickness, you probably wouldn't want to wish that on anyone else. Your puppy might feel homesick in the night but necessarily doesn't have to.

I always had my puppies closer to my bed so they would feel my presence. Luckily, they rarely cried and it can be one of the proven recipes to prevent homesickness. I am often very keen to recommend this approach to anyone who has bought a new puppy.

Puppies generally cry in the night when all settles down and they start to miss their mother. A good trick I also find effective is placing a warm bottle of water in the puppy's bed. That bottle will imitate the warmth of her mother.

If you think that puppies can be homesick just at night, you would be surprised. Puppies can cry during the day too. If your puppy shows any kinds of homesickness and unhappiness, you might fix that by going through this list.

1. Always make sure your puppy has somewhere comfortable to sleep and rest. Buy a dog bed and place it somewhere cozy. Your dog should never be forced to sleep with you in your bed, but if you'd like to do that, make sure that the dog always has a safe place to retreat to if they need it.

2. Never go too far from home without your dog. Many dogs experience homesickness when they are separated from home, and this is unlikely to change. As you are the leader of the pack now, your puppy will look up to you as their god/goddess. The more time you spend together with your dog, the better. As you have already discovered, the contact between the two of you helps you bond better.

3. Remember that dogs are like children too, and they can also experience homesickness and need reassurance. Give your puppy lots of attention, with lots of hugs and cuddles (after all, it's all about love). This should help both you and your puppy feel better, as well as ensuring that there's less of a chance for stress for the animal.

4. Try playing music in the background while you're out of the house. This will help keep your dog occupied, wondering, and curious about what other people might be there.

5. Remember, puppies are very sensitive and can feel human emotions. No matter how upset you are, your dog

needs reassurance from you at a time like this. Don't argue or don't fight in front of your puppy. It is the same as with a human baby. Try to keep the energy clean and solve any problem away from anybody else. When your puppy displays signs of stress, smile and assure them that everything is fine.

Wow, another chapter behind you. You discovered all you need to prepare before bringing the puppy home, you learned about how to safely get the puppy home, and what the first day should be like. You also know how to prevent or treat a puppy's homesickness.

Your puppy is now home with you and that is an excellent time to start with training. In the next chapter, you will learn everything about the art of positive reinforcement and its importance. You will discover different types of dog training and I will teach you over 10 basic commands for your puppy, so you can start raising an amazing pet partner. So go ahead and turn to the next page.

CHAPTER 4

Puppy is Home, Training is on

Now that you understand how to be the strong pack leader that your puppy needs, it is time that you learn the importance of positive reinforcement, which is a method you will use to teach your puppy basic obedience. Since this book is about raising and training your puppy with love, the training method of positive reinforcement has been proven to be kind and very effective.

Training with positive reinforcement is rooted in the old saying 'You can catch more flies with honey than with vinegar.' Your puppy wants to please their alpha, and using that as a training method makes life easier and much more pleasant for both of you!

Art of Positive Reinforcement

Positive reinforcement is truly an art. It combines a gentle way to train your puppy with precision timing. Positive reinforcement rewards a dog for behaving in the expected manner, but refrains from using loud voices or physical approaches otherwise. There's no real 'punishment' for bad behavior. Punishment is negative reinforcement. If it's not the desired behavior, it's ignored as much as possible. Attention, even negative attention, reinforces bad behavior. Treats, attention, and snuggling can only be achieved by giving the behavior that was desired by the alpha.

There is a solid scientific basis to why positive reinforcement is very effective as a training method. Dogs are creatures of habit. They value routine and look for patterns in their day-to-day activities. They learn about their companions and environment in the same way a toddler or child does—by repetition.

This means that if a puppy is consistently rewarded for behaving in a certain way, it will continue following that behavioral pattern until it becomes a habit. Therefore, sooner or later, you will not have to reward your puppy for good behavior every time they perform it, because it simply becomes their second nature to behave that way. Positive reinforcement is a humane and non-threatening way to teach any desired behaviors. It also shows puppies and dogs alike that their human family, and especially their alpha, can be trusted, and that prevents stress and helps them to feel safe.

Confidence, and not fear, is instilled alongside the good habits that form whenever an owner uses positive training methods. Canines are very intelligent and positive reinforcement makes them use that intelligence. They are challenged to figure things out and sometimes you can almost see the wheels turning in their heads.

It is important to note that dogs are very good at reading body language, so controlling your physical expressions is important. It's a natural form of communication for them. Dogs use ear and tail position, as well as whole body stance, to let each other know friendliness, challenge, willingness to fight, protectiveness, and pack position. Don't be surprised if your puppy goes belly up—the position of submission— when they meet someone or another dog. They are just acknowledging that they totally outrank them and they accept it! Make sure that your body language is positive in order to send them the correct messages.

Other desired behaviors can be achieved the same way. If sitting gets a smile and a treat and jumping up doesn't get anything, guess whose butt will start hitting the floor regularly! When you begin house-training, also begin teaching the basic commands, especially 'sit.' Make that pup sit to get a treat, sit to get their meals, and sit before playtime or petting. In a pack, nothing is free; rewards are earned. Be the alpha who demands and rewards acceptable behavior.

When training your puppy, if there is a reasonable situation and command you give it, always impose it. Don't just pass that with a smile and hug your puppy. That is just reinforcing their disobedience and you are losing respect in the puppy's eyes. You, as a leader of a pack, the alpha must be respected and that only happens if your puppy listens to you when you need it.

One of the most important training you will need is leash training. If you don't want to be dragged behind your dog, get a leash tangled between your legs and jumping the puppy from one side to another, then keep on reading. Let's have a look at how to use the art of positive reinforcement when training your puppy on a leash.

Indoor Potty Training

An indoor dog potty could be very beneficial to your household, especially with a new puppy. While you still need to train your dog to use a bathroom outside, indoor bathroom solutions still have a place during sticky situations like living in a high-rise apartment, not having too much time on hand, or not being physically capable of walking your puppy every 2-3 hours or simply cold weather.

Either way, potty training can help you solve some of these issues, but should not be the number 1 way to teach your puppy to excrete. There are many types of dog potties from fake grass to self-cleaning potty pads. It all depends on what you prefer and how much you are willing to spend. Dogs don't like doing their business in a place they sleep. It is against their natural instinct However, as a puppy, this will take a while for them to realize what is their territorium and what is not, and that is why indoor potty training makes it possible.

How to do Indoor Potty Training

Puppies develop their habits very quickly, so showing them where to go and what to do is the fastest way to success.

Your puppy will create a great association with doing their business outside, but in this case also inside if they have the urgency but can't go outside.

1. Create a desired potty place in a different spot than where the puppy sleeps
2. Introduce a potty mat to your puppy by being there with them, making positive associations through play and treats
3. Wait until they excrete
4. Praise them with love, and reward them with a treat

Puppies necessarily don't have to excrete right away when you are there with them but remember, that dogs are incredibly intuitive. Maybe your puppy will get it right the first time, maybe it will take a while but sooner or later, they will create a positive association with going to excrete in a desired place. As I said, don't take it as the main solution. Your puppy needs to be walked and socialized, however, this solution can still be in hand if your puppy urgently needs to go potty right away.

Leash Training

Loose leash walking

New puppy will be pulling you on a leash and it would be a miracle if it didn't. Leash pulling occurs when your dog is excited and wants to move faster than you. It gets a bit difficult to catch up with the speed of your dog as it naturally possesses a faster pace than humans.

It is necessary to train your pup to retain leash manners as it can get stressful for you. It could also lead your dog to tug hard and let loose, which is the last thing you want.

By training your dog to prevent excessive leash pulling, you will have the comfort of walking at a sustained pace, while your dog will pause along with you or wait for your permission to relieve itself at a particular spot.

I want to offer you a few effective tips and tricks for this training, which will help you keep your puppy under total control while on a leash.

Get the right accessories

Uninformed dog owners would simply buy a leash without knowing the types out there, and the effect it would have on their dogs. Get more information on the type of collar, harness, and leash that would be suitable for your dog, according to its size and breed, or ask for help. I recommend using a regular leash and a no-pull dog harness if your puppy tends to have this problem.

Use rewards

Occasional rewards in the form of treats or a favorite toy are useful in garnering your puppy's attention. Use it while you train your puppy on a leash. Walking one step at a time—while holding your puppy's attention using a reward—will make it magically adapt its movement to you.

The command you use for this kind of situation is "With me". If a puppy keeps walking right next to your left leg, keep encouraging them by saying "good boy/girl". Show control and say "no" when it insists on moving forward by tugging at the string. Once it calms down, praise it and offer a treat. This will slowly build an instinct in it to follow your orders, especially when on a leash.

Remember, in training, it is always better to keep it shorter than longer. I will rather train my puppy multiple times a day for 5 minutes than mocking them 30 minutes in a row. Firstly, it is still a puppy and has tons to discover in this world. Secondly, a puppy will lose interest because the span of its attention is short.

Important tip: Practice away from people. The more people and objects, the bigger distraction it is for your puppy. You want to train your puppy somewhere secluded if possible so you can get their maximum attention.

Stand still and change direction

If your puppy keeps on pulling, use tactics like standing still or changing direction. When your dog starts pulling, be glued to the spot for a while and then turn around to walk in the opposite direction. This will make it realize that its behavior is unacceptable, and that it doesn't get what it wants by pulling.

Pulling on the leash is a behavioral problem that will take time to augment, so be patient and consistent in training. Some dogs are significantly more energetic than others, so it might be a good idea to resort to professional training if that is the case with your pup. No matter what your special case is, though, remember that pulling harder on the leash in return will only be counterproductive, so keep a calm and assertive attitude and don't try to solve this problem with muscle strength.

Another way to use the art of positive reinforcement is clicker training. Clicker training is an optional method that will work for most dogs, and the simple idea is to replace treats for clicks, and it works best when transitioning your dog from treat rewards into click rewards.

Clicker Training

For many puppies, a clicker is a great way to train them. Small and inexpensive, clickers work by capturing your dog's attention with an audible sound. You'll use the clicker with a voice command, and if they do the right thing then you'll give your puppy a treat.

Benefits of a Clicker

This method helps to stop your dog from being dependent on the treats and still listen to you. You won't have to call or yell at your puppy, and they can hear the clicker at a long range. This makes it easier to train them to your voice, and your puppy will start to look to you for leadership more quickly.

Simply press the clicker's button when your puppy does what you want them to do and follow the click with a positive reward, such as a small treat or an enthusiastic, encouraging pet, a scratch behind the ears, and a "good boy/girl!" verbal reinforcement.

Step by Step Process

Here is a step-by-step on how to train your dog using a clicker. Make sure you get a clicker that works well to get started.

How To Raise A Puppy with Love

1. Use a Command: You have to start off with a goal in mind. What behavior do you want to target first? One of the best ones to target is "sit". Raise your hand up with a treat visible in it and tell your puppy to sit.

2. Give a Treat: Make sure that you give the treat once they are in the right position. You don't want to have too long of a delay or this will hurt the association process.

3. Repeat: Do it all over again, and make sure that you use the same movement along with the same tone.

4. Vary Reward: Do it a few more times, and once you do you'll need to vary the reward you're giving them. Sometimes, just pet them, sometimes say "good boy/girl!" and sometimes use a treat.

5. Clicker: Once the puppy has already made the association, that's when the clicker comes in. Repeat the process of asking them to sit, then press the clicker's button, and follow the click with a positive reward, such as a small treat or an encouraging pet. They don't know what the new noise is yet.

6. Repeat: This time you're going to tell your dog to sit, holding the clicker and treat over their head. Remember to click it as you lift it up. Give them a treat. Keep repeating.

7. Clicker: Use just the clicker, and if your dog sits give them a treat. You don't have to use words now.

Make sure that you never train your dog in a way where the clicker just gets their attention. You need to assign It to a certain command. Keep in mind that some dogs will learn slower than others, and you can't expect your puppy to learn to respond to the clicker in just a day or two.

When you teach your dog another command with the clicker, then you need to vary the clicking. One-click may be "sit", but two rapid clicks will need to be something like "lie down". However, if you want to add another such as "stay," you can use either three rapid clicks or two slow clicks. If you have a hard time with your puppy not wanting to listen, try giving them a break. Just like kids, they sometimes need to go out for recess, and school can't be every single day.

Essential Commands

There are many different theories about how to train a puppy. Some people believe in firmness and strict commands that come with consequences. Other schools of thought will tell you that providing rewards for good behavior and taking away rewards for bad behavior is the best way to train a puppy. The best course of action really depends on your dog and the animal's specific personality. Some puppies will be interested in pleasing you and others will not really care what you think. The best way to approach obedience training with your puppy is to use consistent practice. Remember that puppies are young and active, so keep your training sessions short and make sure they are not hungry or tired.

"Heel"

Teaching your puppy how to heel is important, especially when there are other dogs around, or people that your dog might want to jump on without invitation. When you command your dog to heel, the dog will sit by your side quietly until released. This is a difficult thing for puppies to learn, especially since they are so energetic and curious by nature. This command is very important when you want to cross the road or just simply keep your puppy by your side.

You can use this command to make your puppy less apprehensive of sounds outside your home. Try doing this exercise while traversing a busy sidewalk. Be vigilant at this point and make sure they heel whenever they feel too curious. Stop walking if they do not listen to you.

The key to this part of puppy training is of course treats. Start by standing with your puppy on a leash and keep a few treats in the hand that isn't holding the leash. The puppy needs to understand the command, so tell your dog to heel. Once they sit still next to you for about five seconds, give the dog a treat. Then, take five steps forward and allow your dog to follow. Say the word "heel" and wait for your puppy to sit down next to you. Reward with a treat. Continue doing this so your puppy understands. The dog will associate your movements and words with the expected behaviors.

Once this is successfully completed in the same location, introduce some other people and distractions. You might feel like you're starting the process all over again, but that's only because your puppy will notice those other people or bouncing balls or moving cars. Repeat the process with the treats until your dog is obedient and able to heel on command.

"Sit"

Use a hand gesture with the "sit" command. The proper hand gesture for this is using the index finger pointing up and towards your puppy. Get your puppy's attention by saying their name, saying the command, and at the same time performing the gesture. Once done successfully, reward immediately. This is my favorite technique, preferably over a Clicker. This process applies for every single command. Sooner or later you will find out that you don't need to speak anymore. You will just use hand gestures and your dog will listen.

For puppies who find it hard to understand the "sit" command, you can tap their rump to bring attention to that body part. Lightly push down to encourage a sitting position and then say the command "sit". Use this method sparingly as your puppy might associate this touching motion as a reward. It should only be used to get an initial reaction.

Teaching your puppy to sit is not complicated, and the dog will understand what you want when you reward it with treats and physically show the animal what you expect. Stand in front of your puppy and hold your hand above its head with a treat in it. They will look up at it. Use your other hand to gently push down on their hindquarters until they are in a sitting position.

At the same time, while still holding the treat, say "sit" in a calm but firm voice. Once they are able to hold the position, give the puppy the treat. Keep repeating this action until the puppy is able to put itself into a sitting position without your guidance. Ultimately, the pup will be able to sit without your help. This is especially useful for greeting situations when you're introducing your dog to new people. Tell the puppy to sit and when that happens, be forthcoming with the treat.

Once your puppy understands what you want without you physically pushing them down, perform the command standing in front of them, commanding verbally, and accompanying them with a gesture.

If your puppy temporarily loses the training you've mastered, simply start again. You might notice your puppy jumps on people when they come into your house or runs after children in the neighborhood. Give the command to sit, and if the dog does not listen, go back to the basics with the treat and the physical lowering of your dog into the sitting position.

"Stay"

The proper hand gesture for this command is with an open palm pointing toward the puppy.

Teaching a puppy to stay might be a little difficult because it's counter-intuitive to a puppy, who wants to explore and jump and sniff and bark. First, designate a spot where you want your dog to stay. That might be a dog bed, a corner of the room, or a particular place that keeps the puppy away from whatever you're doing.

Give the command to "stay" and use your hand gesture at the same time. Continue to repeat the word "stay" so your puppy knows to associate that word with the command. Praise the puppy when you get the obedience you're looking for and the dog stays at the spot you have designated. Wait 10 seconds and reward your pup with a treat.

"Come"

The proper hand gesture for this command is with an open palm placed on the middle of your chest.

Puppies always want to come when they're called. They want to know what you're up to and they're going to be eager to be close to you and be a part of whatever you're doing. However, it can be difficult to get your puppy to come if the puppy is preoccupied with something else.

Maybe the puppy is digging in the backyard or stalking a squirrel or completely obsessed with the scent on some random car's tires. The trick is to teach the dog that coming to you is the best decision that could ever be made. When you call your puppy's name and your little buddy comes running over, shower that dog with praise, love, and treats. With that kind of affection and positive reinforcement, your puppy will never want to miss the opportunity to come to you when called.

For training purposes, call your puppy from one room to another. Stand in the kitchen, when your puppy is in the living room, and call the dog by name and use the hand gesture at the same time. When your puppy comes running, get excited, pet them and provide a treat. When the puppy is able to understand that coming when called means only positive things, they will obey immediately.

Pro Tip: Some puppies might be hesitant to come as they might see you as a large, tall person which might signal a potential danger. If for whatever reason your puppy wouldn't listen to this command, try to bend in your knees and lower yourself. Then perform the command with the hand gesture. This way you appear as a lesser threat to the puppy psychologically, since you are smaller and shorter. That should work perfectly.

"Lie Down"

The proper hand gesture for this command is with an open palm pointing towards the ground when you start at a level of your lower chest and go down to the level of your navel.

Training your puppy to lie down is similar to the way you trained the dog to sit. Find a spot that you want the dog to associate with lying down. That will likely be a dog bed or a mat. Pat the place with your hand and say the words "lie down." If you need to, lower your dog's body to the floor so the puppy understands what lying down means. Reward the final act with a treat as usual. Keep practicing until your puppy gets it. Your puppy might have some of its own ideas about where the best places to lie down are. Respect that instinct and train the pup to lie down in the places that they seem most comfortable.

"Stand"

It is the opposite of the "lie down" command. The proper hand gesture for this command is with an open palm pointing towards the sky when you start at the level of your navel and go up to the level of your lower chest.

This command is used when your puppy is lying on the floor and you want them to get up. Or might be used when your puppy sits and this is the command that tells them to stand back. Very simple, use any type of reward when the command is done successfully.

"Take It"

There is no hand gesture required while performing this command. You and your puppy might appear in a situation where you can through this command encourage your puppy to "take it". This could be taking something out of your hand, or taking something from the floor. Easy, just keep talking to your puppy, sooner or later they will understand.

"Drop it"

There is no hand gesture required while performing this command either. However, this is a very important command. A situation where your dog chews something which can be dangerous to them when swallowing, is not any fun. "Drop it" can be used in all kinds of situations. It commands that whatever the puppy has in its mouth, it must drop it now! You can train this command with a chewing toy. Optionally, you can point your finger and touch the surface where you want the object to be dropped.

"No"

The proper gesture for this command is simple. Your head moving from right to left will do. As you would gesture to a human, this is the same situation.

Puppies don't know right from wrong and if you want them to stop chewing, biting, jumping, or barking, you need to train them to understand the word "no." When your puppy does something you don't like, say the word "no" in a firm, loud voice. If the puppy obeys, reward with a treat.

Redirect the puppy to something else you want them to do. For example, if they are chewing on a piece of clothing, say "No" and give them a toy after that. Again, consistency and patience are absolutely required. You probably won't be able to train your new puppy overnight.

However, with time and structure, obedience training can be conquered.

"Shake"

This command is not truly necessary for basic obedience, but it is easy to perform. Let your puppy sit and while they are sitting, point with your finger on their paw and say "shake". If your puppy lifts their paw, catch it and gently shake it saying "Good boy/girl". and immediately reward them with a treat. If you are not successful with pointing your finger, you can go ahead and touch the paw you want your puppy to lift. That might help your puppy to better understand what you want them to do.

Benefits of Training Games and Activities

Having fun with your puppy through games and activities can always be pleasurable. It can reinforce your relationship with your puppy and further develop how your puppy communicates with you. Certain training games are an extraordinary method for teaching your puppy everything from healthy habits to life-saving abilities. You don't necessarily have to use only games to teach your puppy basic obedience. These are just for entertainment and variety so you can both take the benefits of it.

Games can generally become a difficult task to master, like helping your pet learn when to sit and stay relaxed. Likewise, you can make it a great learning experience for your dog if you choose the right method to teach them all the games. Establishing a positive learning environment is significant for your puppy's health and shows that learning does not need to be boring or include tedious drills. Some of the advantages of utilizing such training games include:

1. Games support your bond with your pet. The relationship you have with your puppy is remarkable. Yet, similar to all other connections, the connection between you and your puppy should be developed further. Your dog must genuinely trust you and ask you out for direction when they are uncertain. Such games assist in building a solid connection between you and your puppy that will extraordinarily work on your association.

2. These games can help you spend a good time together. The more fascinating the training, the more intrigued your puppy will be. And, if your puppy is happy, it will naturally make you cheerful. You can make the training useful by keeping your attitude positive while managing the training.

3. Some training games further develop communication skills. The more we practice and show our puppies new abilities, the better they get at what is generally anticipated and how to talk with us. Likewise, you will understand your

puppies' inconspicuous non-verbal communication by finding out when they are energized, or feeling tired, etc. Games benefit both of you. Correspondence is a two-way road, and you both need to figure out how to see each other's necessities and needs.

4. These games are fascinating, and training should be enjoyable. When it becomes enjoyable for both the trainer and the trainee, you can consistently expect more effective results. After a training session, if the odds are good, you will feel more connected with your pet. Games help your puppy learn everything quickly and thoroughly.

5. An instructional course is not only fun, yet it allows your puppies to have the opportunity to utilize their psychological power, which consumes a great deal of energy. Indeed, showing your puppies something new can be tiring for your little pet simply in an unexpected way.

You will need to follow some significant principles when playing different games, just like any training you perform. Following are a few things that will assist with making learning fruitful for your little pet:

1. End instructional meetings with some playtime. Studies have shown that finishing instructional meetings with a touch of play can help your puppy better hold any new data they have learned.

2. Make sure your pet is in a good position to practice or participate in any activity or game. Do not take your puppy to any public place or area like a park to perform any tricks before making sure that they have mastered the trick effectively at home.

3. You should always give priority to your pet's well-being. If your pet is not prepared to be off-chain, make sure you pamper them with love and tell them that it is fine to be off-chain. If your pet has a past filled with asset monitoring, putting your hand on their toy might prompt a nibble, and is not protected. Take care of your environmental factors and the puppy's health before starting the training. Check the room (or place where you are training) well before starting your training session. This is done to make sure there is no such thing in the room that may cause any kind of harm to your pet.

4. Games should not keep going for the whole day. Games should only be held for a short period of time. Otherwise, your little puppy will get tired from playing too many games in a single day. It is additionally great to end on a high note, so keep games quick and painless.

What games to play

1. **Hide and seek** - This game is fantastic because it is engaging for the puppy and at the same time you are practicing the commands "sit", "stay" and "come". Initially, you might need another person to play this game with you. Let somebody hold the puppy and you go and hide. Once hidden, use the command "come" and let the other person release the puppy. When the puppy finds you, praise them with love.

2. **Find a treat** - Let somebody hold the puppy. Use some nicely smelly treat and let the puppy smell it, but don't let them eat it. Go to another room and hide a treat somewhere visible. Say the command "Find it" and keep encouraging your puppy until they find it. Praise with love. (You can do exactly the same with the puppy's favorite toy for a variety)

3. **Fetch** - Initially, you want to be with your puppy alone without any distractions. Take your puppy's favorite toy, throw it and use the command "Fetch". You might have to go with your puppy towards the toy to help them understand what you want. Once your puppy grabs it, return back, clap with your hands, and command "Come" using a hand gesture you have already learned. Your puppy should return back

to you. Once your puppy gets back to you, command it "Drop it". Then do it all over again.

Training should be entertaining. Our puppies are constantly learning, even at home when we order them to sit. So, learning can happen at any place by combining different day-to-day activities and play.

Teaching Your Dog to be Social Friendly

Consider a four-month-old puppy with no social experience! My friend adopted a little female Pomeranian that had zero social life. She was a very lonely and shy puppy. They could not wait another week to take her outside but they did not know where to begin with her. I gave them a few tips, and boom… problem solved! We decided to walk her down the street twice a day to acquaint her with cars, traffic noises, smells, and people for a very short period of time. Every single day we slightly prolonged the exposure time until she started to feel and look better around other dogs, people and objects. This took another 3 weeks before many puppy lovers could come to say hello, pet her and she enjoyed it. This shows how long socialization training can take for a dog.

Raising a puppy to be socially friendly and acceptable is the second most significant objective of training a pet at home. Keep in mind that stopping them from biting is consistently the main objective. Yet, during your little puppy's first month at home, it is very important to help them socialize with the individuals around them.

Your pup should be completely associated with different individuals around them before they are three months old. Many individuals think that puppy training sessions should ideally be conducted where your dogs can start mingling with other individuals. Not really because it cannot give prolonged benefits. Training is very important for the helpful socialization of little dogs with other individuals as well as different pups.

When and how to prepare your pets?

Discipline sometimes becomes significantly more counterproductive in managing puppies. These pets are extremely autonomous, and discipline can also just scare them. It will require tolerance since puppies learn best through reiteration. Nonetheless, it does not take a lot of time before the puppy starts to be considerably friendlier than previously. You can start by giving little treats for good social behaviors that you demand from your dog.

We all want our puppies to be extremely social, making things easier for us. The thought is to have a pet that is not excessively aggressive yet is ready to associate with different creatures and people without any problem. Having an unsocial pet is quite troublesome. Following are some steps you can follow to make sure you are raising a socially friendly puppy:

1. Indulge your puppy in a social setup

Social training for a dog should begin at the pup stage. It is essential to have the little puppy indulge with individuals when they are twelve weeks old or simply any first day you brought them home. A simple method for doing this is to acquaint pets with as many individuals as expected. This method helps the puppy figure out how to be agreeable around individuals and not bite them in fear. You can ask the visitors to provide treats to your puppy so the puppy can indulge with them as quickly as possible.

2. Find some easy-going animal friends for your little dogs

Puppies can go overboard when they meet different pets. Such encounters can also be sometimes problematic. Such unfriendly conduct from your puppy can be because of their dread of other animals. The puppy may not know how to comprehend the other animal's intentions, and the natural response then, at that point, is to become aggressive. So, to resolve such issues, we need to associate our pups with other animals when they are quite small to acquire better social abilities

3. Help your puppy in indulging with kids

Little dogs are bound to figure out how to acknowledge and be okay with different individuals and circumstances if they are acquainted with them during this time. Make sure your pet meets various animals of different ages in different circumstances if possible. The youngsters at your home should be polite and considerate towards your puppy as well if you have any. If your puppy has great encounters with kids, it will connect them with positive sentiments. On the off chance that you have a grown-up pet, you can help them mingle around kids. The cycle of socialization should go in a leisurely and tender manner. Try to offer a lot of important treats to your pet for their good attitude towards kids.

4. Keep it positive

An ideal way to construct a decent connection between your pet and other people is to utilize encouraging feedback at the point when your puppy is acting admirably around people. Make sure to give it bunches of applause, treats, and consideration. Your pet will discover that beneficial things happen when people are near.

Becoming a Great Trainer - Take Away

Take your dog for a walk regularly

There is nothing that a dog loves more than taking a walk. Taking a walk can give them the exercise they need to wean off their excess energy. Taking a walk also gives them some structure which should emphasize your role as the alpha in your relationship with them. Take your dog out for a walk once or twice a day. A 30-minute walk should be enough to tire your dog out.

Play with your dog

After your training sessions, make it a point to play with your dog. Training can only go so far and your dog will need to play to keep them happy. Throwing a ball for them to chase or wrestling with your dog is a good way of playing with them.

Train your dog in a place free from distractions

You want your puppy's full attention on you at all times during the training session. So, make sure you do your training initially in an environment away from distractions.

Get to know your dog better

One way to become a better trainer is to get to know your puppy better. They are individuals and they have their own unique traits. Use these unique traits to your advantage.

Some puppies can be trained to do certain tricks faster if they have a natural inclination to perform the trick. For example: giving a paw can be reinforced if your puppy raises their paw to get your attention. To do this, simply give them the command "Shake" whenever they raise their paw to reach out to you. Make sure you give them a reward to associate it with good behavior.

Time your training sessions

Quality over quantity is the key to having a great training session. Keep your training sessions short so that you can maintain your puppy's motivation and attention.

Studies have shown that keeping your training sessions under 15 minutes shows better results than training sessions that take longer. Make sure that you focus each training session on a certain command until they fully understand it and then complement the training session with other commands that they are already familiar with.

Be the leader of the pack

In the wild, wolves and dogs form packs as a form of security. Young puppies learn by imitating the actions of the older dogs in the pack. They are also corrected immediately if they do not follow instructions immediately.

This is basically the same thing within your home. To effectively train your puppy, be the leader of the pack.

Reward your dog's good behavior

To encourage good behavior, always make sure that you reward your dog. Be mindful of what they are doing and always keep a treat on you or nearby so you can immediately heap them with rewards for good behaviors.

Doing this several times should help them form an association in their mind that this type of behavior is rewarded and they will do it constantly to get the treats in your hand.

Timing is the key

Proper timing should be practiced at all times so you can catch your puppy if they are doing something good or bad. It goes without saying that proper behavior should be rewarded while negative behaviors should be corrected to the desired one.

Never reinforce undesirable behavior

Some negative behaviors puppies do may seem cute and harmless during their early years. This should never be reinforced as it could become a big problem in the future.

Excessive play barking for instance is one type of behavior that may seem cute. Now imagine your puppy as a grown-up dog with a louder bark. If they get excited they are going to bark and it can be a nuisance for you and your neighbors if they bark incessantly during playtime.

Training your dog is a day-to-day activity

Training your dog is not something that you do on a whim. This is part of your ongoing commitment to raising your puppy right.

This means you will have to train your pup daily. Sometimes casually, sometimes in scheduled 5-15 minutes blocks. Training your dog daily makes it an activity for your dog to look forward to. This ensures that they are always motivated and will keep their mind from getting bored.

Use one-syllable word commands at the beginning

Use one-syllable word commands so that your dog easily understands what is expected of them. If you've noticed, the basic commands are one-syllable words. Treat it as an emulation of how your pup would interact with another dog in the pack. Dogs communicate using short barks or yelps to tell one another what to do.

Focus on one command at a time

Focus on one command at a time to make it easier for your puppy to understand what it is you want them to do. As soon as they learn the lesson by heart, mix it up to check for further understanding.

Recognize the fact that all dogs are different

One great thing about dogs is that they come in all shapes and sizes. They also come with specific personalities and quirks. But, there is a good way to gauge what your dog is capable of doing by learning more about the breed and the class they belong to.

Here's a basic rundown of breeds and classes and other pertinent information:

The sporting group

This is a great breed for people who live an active lifestyle and want to own a puppy that can reflect the same amount of energy. The sporting group is easy to train as they are highly motivated to perform and they have the energy to match their eagerness.

Expect these dogs to do well with walking exercises related to training and fetching stuff.

The hound group

These are the seekers in the dog world equipped with the most powerful noses. These dogs do well in situations where they have to find something and bring it back to you. Play to this breeds strengths by keeping them occupied with tricks and training exercises that engage their sense of smell.

These dogs are also very easy to entice with treats as their powerful noses can smell hidden treats in your palm or in containers hidden from view.

The working group

These dogs easily get bored if they don't have anything to do. These dogs thrive well in training situations as it gives them something to focus on. Their high energy and motivation levels will also help them last through longer training sessions than most dogs.

Working dogs are fun to work with because they are very eager to learn and please their master. They are also highly capable of learning complex tricks that other groups may not be able to learn easily.

A downside to having a working dog is their tendency to become destructive when they get bored. So make it a point to give them regular exercise and training sessions so you won't end up with a destroyed home.

The terrier group

This group is a fun bunch as they are always amped. These dogs have very high energy levels and are on par with that working dog's energy level.

Terriers are also very eager to please and thrive in training situations. In fact, terriers are often lumped in with working dogs because these little pups love to perform specific chores like hunting and chasing down balls and other moving toys.

Give them as much exercise as a working dog and you should have a very contented terrier snoring by your side at night. Don't expect them to sleep soundly though, because any sound (no matter how faint it may seem) is bound to get them up and alert within seconds to investigate!

The toy group

The toy group is often thought of as lazy dogs but this is far from the truth as most of the dogs lumped into this category also belong to the terrier group.

The toy group can be very energetic but they do tire out easily because of how their bodies are built.

Still, that's no excuse to not give them some form of exercise.

Dogs belonging to the toy group are very territorial so you will have to make sure that you weed out their aggressive tendencies by socializing them properly. Do not fall for their charms as you might end up with a dog who is jealous of anyone else giving you attention.

Dogs belonging to the toy group are also incessant barkers so make sure you address this by using the spray method to keep them from barking without any reason for hours on end.

The non-sporting group

These dogs are perfect for people who have very low energy levels. These dogs love to lounge around and just stay chill.

Teach these dogs the basic commands but don't expect them to follow immediately.

These dogs would rather sleep than fetch a ball. So keep your training sessions short enough to keep their attention on you and leave them alone for the rest of the day.

Since these dogs tend to get fat from the lack of activity, make it a point to put them on a strict diet and to give them some minimal exercise to keep them healthy.

The herding group

This is an offshoot of the working dog group. Treat these dogs like working dogs and you won't have any issues with destructive tendencies.

The mixed breed group

The view on mixed breeds has changed over the course of time and people are now more open to adopting mixed breeds instead of just purebred dogs. Mixed breed dogs appear to be stronger than their counterparts and have better overall health than purebreds.

It is also fun getting to know a mixed breed because you'll never know what you'll get. They may retain certain characteristics from one or two parents and their personalities may also be a mixture of their predecessors.

Make it a point to research both breeds that your mixed breed belongs to so that you have a good idea of what to expect and then train them according to their natural strengths.

Learn more about your dog

If you want to get to know your dog better, take the time to learn more about them. There are many educational materials that can help point you in the right direction. You can visit your local library and check for books specifically targeted at the breed or you can scour the internet for every tidbit of information that can help you know more about your dog.

There are many types of dogs and each specific breed comes with its own specific quirks. You can use the information you learn to address their weaknesses and play to their strengths. This should in turn make training an easier process because you have a better understanding of what makes your dog tick.

Watch expert trainers do their work

Reading about training methods can only take you so far. You might want to enhance your innate talent in training dogs by learning from the experts.

Watch how expert dog trainers operate and take note of how they train their dogs and emulate what they are doing.

Better yet you can contact an expert dog trainer and ask them to teach you how to train your dog properly. You may have to pay them for their services but learning how to properly train your dog is something that is priceless!

Don't flick your dog's nose

Have you ever had your nose hit? It stings right?

That's basically the same for your puppy. Except dogs' noses are more sensitive to human beings. Dogs' noses are full of nerves and cavities which makes them an efficient tool for finding hidden stuff or recognizing one another.

Flicking your puppy's nose is a very traumatic event and your puppy will remember the pain associated with it. This may build some distrust between you and your puppy which could impede your training progress.

So, never, ever flick your dog's nose.

Last but not the least: **Love your dog and your dog will love you**

This is the most important part of owning a dog. Give your puppy lots of love and you can be sure that they will give you back the same amount of love if not more! There is nothing that can compare to a dog's love for its human. It is an unconditional love that nothing short of death can stop.

So now you know how to become a great trainer. We have discussed everything from the method of positive reinforcement, and leash and clicker training, to learning 10 basic commands and games you can play with your puppy for their further development and deeper connection between the two of you. In the next chapter, we will discuss your puppy's health and how to care for them. Health is wealth and that applies to us humans as well as to our dogs. There are things you need to know in order to keep your dog active, healthy, and with the highest chance of a long and happy life. Are you ready? Let's go.

CHAPTER 5

Puppy's Health & Care Basics

The care you give to your puppy will determine how healthy and vibrant it will be in the future. As I said multiple times in this book, it is your responsibility and commitment to care for your puppy as best as you possibly can. Yes, there are instances where health issues can be inevitable, for example, inherited disease. I don't want to scare you, these things happen but you will very likely have a beautifully healthy puppy, and this chapter is made for you to make sure that they stay that way. I truly believe that your dog will have an amazing, long, and vibrant life by your side.

Let's check the basic health & care for your puppy so you and your little pooch can be worry-free.

Puppy Proofing

While certain breeds of dogs might have a reputation for being bitter or having other undesirable traits, nurture has a lot of influence on your puppy's behavior. If you are bringing home a 6-8 week old puppy, you are bringing home a baby. Their little brain is immature, and this baby will get into mischief if left unsupervised.

Young pups can get into a lot of things – even if you have carefully puppy-proof your home. Furthermore, they grow at a rapid rate. Items that seemed safe at first can quickly become a hazard as your little one becomes bigger and stronger. You will need to be vigilant to protect your pup and your possessions from each other. Hide anything that seems dangerous and if possible, don't leave any small objects on the ground. I know that might be hard, especially if you have little kids. However, puppies tend to chew almost anything they can find and that is not good news for us as owners.

My friend Monica has a 5-year-old Labrador Retriever, Jessy. Labradors really tend to chew all kinds of things. Monica has a child of the same age. She is generally very diligent in cleaning, but sometimes things get out of control. Her child played with a lego one afternoon and left it dirty in the backyard. An unattended Jessy unfortunately swallowed a couple of those pieces. Monica didn't find out immediately, but later in the evening because Jessy wasn't able to properly empty herself.

Monica thought that was weird and decided to keep an eye on Jessy overnight.

The next morning Jessy was having problems pooping again, and shortly after that, she started having stomach cramps, and not looking very well. Monica took Jessy to the veterinary clinic where she had to have surgery and took the lego pieces out of her stomach. That procedure cost almost $2000. This happened 2.5 years ago.

One year after that the same situation happened again. Jessy swallowed little rocks and she couldn't excrete them. The same procedure, another almost $2000. Jessy is fine now but can you imagine? I couldn't believe what Monica was saying to me. And Jessy wasn't even a puppy by this time. Please always make sure your home is safe so you can prevent such things before they happen.

Daytime Pet Care

If you have a family member who is home most of the day, that is an ideal situation when bringing home a new puppy. If there is no one at home during the day, you might want to arrange daytime care for your baby. This could be a neighbor who comes in to feed and walk your infant doggie, or you could take your pup to doggie daycare.

Remember, a puppy needs to socialize and bond, mostly with you as a leader of the pack. That means, make sure to personally spend as much time as you possibly can around your puppy, and if you are not there, let somebody else be with them. Don't get me wrong, a puppy needs to learn how to be on their own so they won't create an addiction on you or somebody else, but that stage will come later, somewhere around 5-6 months old. Until that time, be around as much as you possibly can.

Feeding

A new puppy needs to be fed at least three times a day – and possibly more. Read labels carefully. Look for the words "complete nutrition" and "sustains growth", as well as the AAFCO seal. "Dog tested" is also a good note on puppy food. Every dog is a little different. A proper diet for your dog's vitality and longevity will vary on a stage of life too.

Go for quality dry food first. That is the basics. You can usually find out on a label which food is suitable for which dog's age. The best is always discussing your pet's diet with a certified veterinary practitioner. As your puppy grows, additionally, you will never get wrong by feeding them a whole foods diet.

Foods such as cooked meat (No Spices!), fruit (except citrus fruit), and vegetables (My dogs love apples, bananas, avocados, carrots, and pumpkin) - Fruit and vegetables also add a good amount of fiber which is great for your dogs' elimination process. For a shine fur, you can add an egg (cooked so you don't have to worry about salmonella)

Foods you should never feed your dog

No salt and salty foods

No chocolate, no sweets, no sugar

No pastry (No bread, No dough, etc.)

No citrus fruit (lemon, grapefruit, orange, or lime)

No milk and lactose products

No onion and garlic

Your puppy would probably eat almost anything you would give it but that doesn't mean it is good and healthy for them. Make sure you feed your dog with quality foods dry and whole foods and as a reward you will get a vibrant, beautiful, and healthy companion.

Eliminating

Your puppy still has a baby-sized bladder, so a trip to the designated potty spot or taking a walk needs to take place about every three hours.

Sleeping and Resting

Like any baby, your puppy will enjoy playing – but will soon follow up with a much-needed nap. This can be in the kennel or maybe snuggled up with you. Even though it might seem as if you are spoiling your puppy, snuggling with you helps promote the pack bonds that your little one needs for healthy mental development.

Your puppy might sleep a little longer at night. But is likely to whimper and cry at bedtime Some schools of thought insist that the puppy should be made to sleep in the kennel or in a basket from the very beginning. However, most puppies will want to sleep with you.

If you choose to confine the pup to the kennel, don't make them go lie down with anything at all. Make sure the bottom liner is clean, dry, and soft. Place a cuddly toy in the kennel, and play some soft music or place an old ticking clock nearby.

If you choose to allow the pup to sleep with you, that is fine. Your puppy is used to sleeping with littermates and mama. Sleeping with you will assist with the bonding process. If they will be a big dog, you might want to encourage sleeping in a basket or bed that is near your bed (as I always did). Make the sleeping bed available during the day for naps and time-outs from activity – particularly if the household includes young children.

Puppy's mental health

As well as humans, dogs also have mental health. The only way you can care for and help your puppy grow into a mentally and physically strong dog is mostly your approach. Always speak to your pup in calm soothing tones. Never yell at the pup or strike them, and don't allow others to do so either. You can be firm without scolding or hitting the dog. Being violent with your dog can have a disastrous effect resulting in fear, shyness, or aggression.

Speaking calmly, and lovingly and petting them gently models the kind of behavior you expect from them. Training a puppy isn't very different from training a young child. Even though dogs' mouths do not allow them to speak human language, they can recognize and understand a vocabulary of more than 200 words – very much like a preverbal child.

Dogs do not enjoy being harshly patted or thumped – as a rule. To them, this treatment is very much like being hit. They like to be stroked in the same direction that their hair grows, especially along the sides of their face. This mimics their natural affection with canine pack members. They also like to be scratched gently in places that collect skin flakes and loose hairs – especially those they cannot easily reach for themselves.

Some dogs will close their eyes, and get a dopey sort of expression on their faces when they are enjoying the attention. Others will make little grunting sounds of pleasure.

Playtime

Puppies and even older dogs love to play. If you provide chew toys, soft toys, and tug toys they will have a good time interacting with you or even playing alone in ways that do not destroy your furniture and home.

Chew toys should either be too tough to tear up or they should be puppy "bones" that are intended to be chomped and shredded to oblivion. These latter toys will need to be replaced often, but will prove a true saving in keeping your pup from tearing up your house and possessions.

Each dog will have its own ideas about what is appropriate in the way of toys. Some like soft cuddly toys, while others enjoy bouncy balls or knotted ropes for tugging. Still, others like a toy that can be thrown and brought back. Highly active dogs like to catch Frisbees or chase balls.

Let your dog tell you which toys they enjoy. As you tune in on your pet's behavior, you will quickly be able to tell which are preferred. For example, one little girl pup loved cuddly toys. She nosed them about in her kennel, organized and snuggled them. On the other hand, an energetic shepherd/lab mix pup loved to run and chase things.

They would proudly bring them back and eagerly sit waiting for the next throw. When left alone with their toys, they would pick up their breath-freshener tennis ball in their mouth, throw it down with enough force that it would bounce, and then they would chase after it. Other dogs like to go up onto high places, or jump over things. The kinds of play your dog enjoys will let you know what sort of tricks they will easily learn.

Shelter

For shelter, a puppy only needs a space big enough for them to turn around, stand up or sit without feeling cramped.

If you plan to have your dog outside, make sure that your dog's shelter or home is sturdy enough to withstand its rambunctiousness and warm enough for them to get comfortable at night. It doesn't have to be fancy. Four walls and a sturdy floor with a soft, warm blanket for a bed should suffice.

Make sure you clean their shelter out every 2 or 3 days and spray it with anti-mite and lice solution to reduce the risk of these bugs bothering your puppy. You can also wash their blanket and place it under the sun to get rid of any lice and mite eggs as well as lessen the puppy dour that's going to develop from constant use.

Grooming

Grooming is essential for your puppy's health and well-being. It is in your best interest to have a clean, healthy, and happy puppy so that you won't have any issues during training.

Maintaining your puppy's fur - Your puppy needs constant grooming (especially if they're the long-haired variety) to maintain its overall health and happiness. Depending on their age, give your puppy a regular bath once or twice a month to keep their fur clean. Make sure you blow dry and wipe them off with a towel to remove excess moisture. A quick brushing session once or twice a week should remove tangles and matted fur but some breeds need brushing daily.

Maintaining your puppy's teeth – You will also have to check their teeth to keep them clean and away from any possible dental issues that could impact their health. You can purchase amazing edible sticks that can serve as a treat and will clean your pup's teeth too.

Maintaining your puppy's claws – your puppy has claws that will grow over time and this can impede their mobility if they grow too long. Make it a point to teach your puppy that clipping their claws is not something to be afraid of.

Extra tip: Make sure you clean your pup's ears roughly once a week, clean their drowsy eyes daily and give them a good bath 1-2 times a month.

Exercise and physical strength

It's a known fact that dogs love to walk. They simply can't live without it. And giving your dog some exercise is an essential part of your relationship with your puppy.

Simply letting your puppy off its leash in your backyard isn't going to be enough. They need a structured exercise more than just a carefree romp in the garden.

Through walks, you can establish your role as the alpha while your puppy faithfully follows at your side or behind you. 30 minutes walk (minimum) should be enough to wean off the excess energy your puppy builds up over time.

Depending on the breed, if suitable, take your dog for a hike, throw them their favorite toy, make them run back and forth, and make them physically active. That will help overall with their health, resilience, and longevity.

Try to match your exercise with the type of breed your dog belongs to. Some dogs need more physical activity than others however you don't want to unnecessarily exhaust your puppy if they are not made for it.

Temperature

It's a terrible feeling when you can sense that your puppy isn't being itself but you're not sure how serious its condition is or what you can do to help. This is why it's important to know how to read your dog's vitals. The more you know about what's normal for your pup, the quicker you can tell when something isn't quite right with it.

Your puppy's temperature is a good indicator of its overall health. It's one of the first things your veterinarian will check when you take your dog for a regular visit. To give your fur baby the best care possible, it's important that you know how to check its temperature, how to interpret the reading, and how to act if it's higher or lower than normal.

What's a puppy's normal temperature?

Normal body temperature can vary from one puppy to another, which is why taking your dog's temperature is important as it tells you what your puppy's "normal" is. Generally, the average temperature for newborn puppies falls between 95° and 99°F. At around three weeks old, your puppy's temperature should range from 97° to 100°F, and after the fourth week, it should have the normal body temperature of an adult dog, which is usually between 99.5° and 102.5°F.

Body temperature over 104°F or under 99°F is an indication of an emergency situation. Extremely high or low temperatures can be fatal for puppies if not treated. So if you take your puppy's temperature and the reading appears to be dangerously high or low, seek veterinary care immediately.

How to check your puppy's temperature

A popular myth surrounding the body temperature of dogs is that you can tell if they have a fever by feeling their noses. If it's cool and wet, then the dog's temperature is normal, but if it's hot and dry, then it has a fever. This is completely wrong; the only accurate way to check your dog's temperature is by using a thermometer.

Ear and mouth temperatures are unreliable in dogs, which means that you'll need a digital or a bulb rectal thermometer to get an accurate reading. If your puppy looks unwell, you need to start with this procedure to check its temperature. It might be easier if you get another person to help you hold your dog in place while you take its temperature.

The procedure will take around a minute, so make sure that your dog is comfortable in its standing position before you start.

Besides the thermometer, you will also need baby oil, mineral oil, or petroleum jelly to lubricate the tip of the thermometer.

To measure the pup's temperature, lift its tail and gently but quickly insert the lubricated thermometer about an inch into its rectum. Press the start button on your digital thermometer and hold it in place until you hear the beep that signals completion. If you're using a bulb thermometer, you won't have to press a button, but you will need to shake down the thermometer until it reads about 96°F before you use it. After you're done with the thermometer, be sure to clean it using rubbing alcohol or a suitable, dog-friendly disinfectant.

If you are unsure in any of those steps, take your puppy to the vet right away. It is better to be safe than sorry. Just bear in mind that if your puppy has a fever, do not, under any circumstances, give it medication at home without consulting your vet. Human medication can be poisonous to dogs and cause severe illness or even death.

Understanding Bowel Movements

Bowel movement isn't a pleasant topic to talk about but it's a very important one; your puppy's stool is a good indicator of its overall health. Keeping an eye on your dog's poop can help you ensure its well-being and alert you in case of a health problem. To better monitor your pet's health, you must understand the signs that differentiate between healthy and unhealthy dog poop.

What should healthy poop look like?

When picking up your dog, there are four main characteristics to look for in its poop: color, content, consistency, and coating. The color of healthy stool should be chocolate brown and there shouldn't be any visible content in it. As for consistency, your puppy's stool should be firm and a little moist, like playdough. Ideally, your pup's stool would be log-shaped with little cracks in it and no coating on it at all. So, if your puppy has medium-brown, semi-firm, coating-free poop with nothing sticking out of it, you have nothing to worry about.

How does your puppy's diet affect its bowel movement?

The volume and odor of the stool are also important to note. Puppies who eat only processed kibble typically excrete large quantities of stinking poop. This is because many dog food manufacturers add high amounts of fiber to their products and your puppy can't process all these nutrients so instead of metabolizing them, its body pushes them out, producing high volume with a strong odor.

Dogs who eat raw and homemade food typically produce significantly smaller stool with a much weaker smell, but if the raw diet is too high in calcium, your puppy may pass white, chalky feces or even suffer from constipation. That is why it is great to combine dry foods with a whole foods diet.

As you can see, what constitutes "normal" poop may vary depending on the pup's diet among other factors. This is why it's important to pay attention to what your dog's stool usually looks and smells like so you'll be immediately aware of any signs of potential diet or health problems.

The most common poop abnormalities

Diarrhea is a common sign of a potential health problem in puppies. The causes of diarrhea typically include viral and bacterial infections, intestinal parasites, food intolerance, allergies, and inflammatory bowel disease. In the case of large bowel inflammation, diarrhea is often accompanied by a coating of mucus. Sometimes that just means that your puppy ate something that wasn't suitable for them. If it is one time off, you have nothing to worry about. If diarrhea continues, don't hesitate and go to the vet.

Another common abnormality is a soft stool with no visible blood or mucus. This is usually a result of either a dietary change or irregular eating. Regardless of the stool's consistency, the presence of red streaks or fresh blood is almost always a sign of a serious health problem that requires immediate attention.

When it comes to your puppy's overall health, what they excrete is as important as what they ingest, and since your furry friend can't tell you when they have a stomach ache or some other digestive problem, it's up to you to stay alert for signs of trouble. So, bring your tolerance levels up and look for the four Cs in your dog's stool: color, content, consistency, and coating.

Wound Care

Puppies are naturally playful, energetic, and inquisitive; all of these traits may lead to accidents resulting in cuts and scrapes at some point in their life. Cleaning the wound properly will prevent infection and help your dog heal quickly if you cover all your bases. Understanding how to assess wounds and treat them is essential for your pup's health.

Stopping the bleeding

Any shallow wound, whether bleeding or not, will require immediate attention to ensure it doesn't get infected. Once you realize your puppy has a wound, the first step is to stop the bleeding. Apply pressure on the wound with a gauze tape or a cloth for a bigger cut.

Cleaning the wound

Once the bleeding has stopped, you need to flush out the wound as soon as possible. You will need to use a saline solution as a first step. You can either use a store-bought saline solution—such as contact lens solution if you have it on hand—or you can make some at home. To make the saline solution, add two teaspoons of salt to one cup of warm water and stir until completely dissolved.

To use the solution, it's best to use a syringe or baster and squirt a large volume of the liquid to bathe or drown the wound in. This is both to disinfect the wound and to clean out any bacteria and debris that might not be noticeable. Keep washing the wound until the tissue is clear and glistening. If the wound is on your pup's tail or paw, keep the solution in a bowl and soak the injured paw or tail for three to five minutes, and then pat dry gently.

What to use

Depending on the severity of the wound, you may want to use a disinfectant as a final rinse or soak. You can dilute a capful of betadine or chlorhexidine in a cup of warm water to use for this purpose.

Unless instructed by your vet, never use hydrogen peroxide, harsh soaps or shampoos, rubbing alcohol, oils, or any other product to clean an open wound, as they may contain substances that are toxic to your puppy or may irritate the wound and inflame it further.

Drying the wound

Once you are sure the wound is clean, you need to dry it. It's a good idea to use a gauze pad because it won't leave any fragments in the wound, but any clean and lint-free material will be fine. Pat the wound gently to avoid causing more pain or injury, then bandage the wound to keep your puppy from licking it. Use a bandage tape around the gauze to hold it in place.

Following up

After you've taken all these steps, it's a good idea to keep checking on the wound daily to see how it is healing. If it seems to be going ok, then just continue to change the bandages regularly until the wound is completely healed. However, if the wound does not close, or starts to emit any smell, you have to contact your veterinarian immediately.

It's important to understand that for small wounds such as scratches and minor cuts, you can easily take care of your puppy at home. However, for any other type of injury that fully penetrates the skin such as bite wounds, deep gashing wounds, or bruises that won't heal, your puppy should receive immediate veterinary attention.

Giving Pills to Your Puppy

Many people think that it's practically impossible to give their pet its pills. And they have all the right to feel this way; after all, you might end up chasing your puppy all around the house. This is when you start to look for new and practical ways to give your little pooch its meds. Thankfully, there are plenty of those you can try—if one doesn't work, the next surely will.

Go old school

I know that doesn't sound the most loving but there are occasions you simply have to do it in the name of love for your puppy. If your little puppy is an easygoing sweetheart, you can simply give it the pill as is. All you need to do is tilt back its head to face the ceiling, then gently open its mouth. After that, you push the pill to the back of its tongue and stroke its throat until you make sure that the pill is swallowed. To double-check, you can give your pup some water in order to be sure that the pill does not get stuck in its throat.

Sneak it in soft or sticky food

Trick 101 to giving your puppy its pills is hiding one in its food. Try sticking the pill in a meatball or a dollop of peanut butter and your pet will swallow it without even noticing that it's there. However, there are also many picky dogs that are very particular about what they eat. These pets are very intelligent and can easily realize that there is a hidden pill in their food (Just like mine). They end up eating around the pill and leave the rest. The good thing about this trick is that there are many types of sticky and soft foods for you to hide the pill in—so you can experiment until you find the one thing that your puppy never seems to refuse.

Use a pill device

Pill devices are one of the very helpful tools created for pets. Using one helps you avoid the hassle of getting your hand bitten just because your puppy is refusing to take its meds and starting to get a little too agitated. All you need to do to use this device is to simply place it as close as you can to the puppy's throat, and drop the pill. After that, close its jaws and gently stroke its throat downwards to make sure that it swallows it.

Puppies are adorable indeed, but they are very smart as well. So, don't underestimate how tricky it can be to convince them to do something they don't want to. However, giving them the right medication can be of vital importance, so it's best to start familiarizing them with this process early on. For example, most worm care comes in pills and that is something we should do on an ongoing basis. This is why you need to make sure that you stay calm and be persistent each time you give your dog a pill—when it knows there's nothing to be afraid of, it'll eventually be happy to cooperate.

Common Illnesses

I am not here to scare you. I am also not saying that something like that will ever happen to your puppy. In fact, I have had 5 dogs in my lifetime (not counting those we had when I was a child) and I was always "lucky" to have a perfectly healthy dog. I believe it is the care you give them, and if you don't underestimate the little details you have read in this book, you will not have any problems either. However, things happen and I want you to be armed with knowledge and prepared if something happens to your puppy.

Puppies can suffer from a lot of the same illnesses and health conditions as adult dogs, but because of their size and age, these illnesses can be a lot more serious in their case. They are more prone to developing diseases as their bodies are not strong enough to combat viruses and bacteria. Here, we list the most common illnesses that can affect puppies that you have to be aware of and keep an eye out for.

Kennel cough

Also known as infectious tracheobronchitis, this illness is characterized by an aggravating and loud cough. It's very contagious and often contracted from crowded places such as dog kennels or pet stores. If your puppy has it, it will need a visit to the vet as soon as possible to get medical treatment, as untreated kennel cough can develop into deadly pneumonia in puppies. If your pooch is abnormally tired, and has a decreased appetite and fever, along with a wheezing cough, then definitely get it checked out. With the right treatment, your puppy should get better within 10 – 14 days.

Canine parvovirus

Another serious illness that is very common among puppies is canine parvovirus (parvo). It typically affects puppies up to four months of age, especially if they haven't received all their vaccinations yet. Parvo is caused by a virus that induces symptoms that start with bloody diarrhea, then it is followed by vomiting, sleepiness, and loss of appetite. If you see any of those symptoms in your puppy, you have to take it to a veterinarian immediately. In this case, your dog will most likely be hospitalized for a few days and then go home with medication to continue treatment.

Canine distemper

Another common disease is distemper, which threatens to affect young puppies that have not yet been vaccinated against it. Unfortunately, puppies who contract this illness are at a high risk of developing permanent neurological damage. Symptoms can include yellow diarrhea, issues with breathing, eye and nasal discharge, and loss of appetite. If your puppy contracts distemper, it will most likely be hospitalized for a few weeks before it can go back home with you.

Hyperglycemia

Especially if you own a toy breed puppy, such as a chihuahua or miniature poodle, you need to be aware that it might be at a high risk of experiencing hyperglycemia during the first year of its life. Toy breeds have tiny stomachs that may not be able to handle long intervals between meals. This causes them to have low blood sugar, and that can have a serious effect on their health—and even become life-threatening. Puppies suffering from hyperglycemia will start being inactive, appear to be spaced out or not focused, and in extreme cases, they will experience seizures and even death. Therefore, young puppies need to be fed every 3 hours on average, and if you feel that your puppy is showing any symptoms of low blood sugar, place a small amount of honey right into its mouth and follow up with a vet appointment right away.

Gastrointestinal issues

Although they're technically not illnesses but rather symptoms, vomiting and diarrhea can be very common indicators of underlying diseases. If your puppy is experiencing either—or both—the first thing to do is rule out a serious case of intestinal parasites. It can also simply be an upset tummy or that your puppy ate too fast or licked something that was not clean. Some puppies might even vomit due to hunger or stress. The severity of GI issues depends on the dog's habits and how long they last. No matter the case, you have to keep your puppy well hydrated for the following 12 hours after vomiting or 24 hours after diarrhea. If your pooch does not get better, then a visit to the veterinarian will be required.

These guidelines are meant to help you know when something is wrong, assess how severe the situation is, and help you provide specific, detailed information to your vet. They're by no means a substitute to veterinary care but may prove useful in determining whether or not your pet needs an emergency visit to the vet.

Dealing with Fleas and Ticks

Fleas and ticks are nightmares for dog owners. There are thousands of pests out there, but a handful can be enough to affect your puppy and bring you misery. Although ticks and fleas are year-round pests, owners tend to encounter them the most during warmer months. These tiny parasites not only irritate your dog, but they also transmit disease and infest your home.

If you and your dog are already scratching your heads, we've got you covered with a list of prevention methods and ways to deal with fleas and ticks.

How to know if your puppy has ticks or fleas

Your puppy will probably be constantly scratching and biting itself along the back and the base of its tail if it's infested with fleas.

Because some dogs are allergic to the flea's saliva, a few puppies will show signs of a severe skin reaction from just a single bite. You might also notice brownish-black fleas moving through your puppy's hair or flea dirt on its coat.

The presence of ticks, however, is harder to detect. Your dog may have several of them attached to its skin without showing any symptoms, so it's very important to examine it closely by parting the fur and running your hands through its skin. Pay special attention to your puppy's face, inside the ears, between the toes, as well as the groin area.

Laying their eggs in bushes or dark, sheltered areas, ticks attach themselves to the skin and feed on blood. Their sizes can range from a poppy seed to a raisin, and it's crucial to remove them as soon as possible, as they can transmit serious diseases.

Prevention methods

Fleas and ticks tend to hate sunlight and stick to dark, hidden areas. However, that doesn't mean your energetic puppy that loves playing outside won't need maximum protection. Especially if you live—or go for hikes—in woody areas, you should be extra careful to protect your fur baby.

Make sure your lawn's grass is short to ensure it gets enough sunlight, and clean up wood piles or fallen leaves regularly to prevent ticks from dwelling there.

For your backyard, you can use nematodes and diatomaceous earth to keep fleas and ticks under control. For the best results, get your dog vaccinated.

Treatment

Even though the preventives will keep the parasites away, you might still need to take more measures to get rid of existing fleas and ticks. The two basic control products are adulticides and insect growth regulators. Adulticides kill adult fleas, whereas the insect growth regulators stop ticks and fleas from maturing. You can also opt for flea shampoos, pills, or powders that kill those insects within hours.

Removing ticks will require tweezers, and it can help if your partner holds the dog as you go through the process. Make sure you grab the tick by its head, as close to the skin as possible, or else its body may be crushed all over your dog, sending toxins into its bloodstream. After removing the tick, place it in a jar filled with rubbing alcohol, as your vet might need to identify the specific type of tick that bit your dog in case of a complication.

To get rid of fleas manually, you'll need a flea comb. Comb your dog's hair thoroughly, and if fleas get stuck in the comb's teeth, place them in soapy water for a while to ensure that they're all dead before you discard them.

Keep your home free from fleas and ticks

After you've treated your dog, you'll still want to make sure the fleas and ticks are out of your home. You'll need to wash all the bedding in hot water, apply non-toxic sprays to your yard, vacuum all your carpets and floors and then throw away the vacuum bag, and continue to treat your dog with the monthly preventives. If you have a serious home infestation at hand, you can go for flea bombs or seek professional help.

It hurts to see your pet in pain. If it's going through a pest infestation, it will likely spend hours every day scratching itself and biting at its paws. If it's prone to allergies, fleas and tick bites may even lead to a weakened immune system, causing a whole lot of other issues. Luckily, though, with constant care, you can get rid of the nuisance of ticks and fleas, and keep them in check for good.

Just for your information. These are the worst-case scenarios. My dogs and many of my client dogs had ticks and never had any health issues after that.

Vaccinations

As your puppy learns to interact with the world, you'll need to take good care of its physical health, and this includes prevention. You'll need to protect your dog from potentially harmful diseases through vaccinations.

When to consider vaccination

A puppy should ideally start taking vaccines as soon as you get it, unless it's a special case. You'll need to continue with your fur baby's booster shots every three weeks until it is four months of age. Vaccinations normally begin after the puppy has been weaned off by its mother.

Remember to schedule your vaccination appointment during your first veterinarian visit, which should take place sometime around the first week of receiving your new pet.

Core vaccines you cannot skip

Some vaccines are required by all dogs, while some others will depend on your pup's lifestyle. Core vaccinations are vital to your puppy's health and well-being.

Canine distemper

As mentioned before, this severe and dangerous virus affects dogs' nervous, respiratory, and gastrointestinal systems, spreading from other infected animals. It can also be transmitted through food or shared equipment. The virus causes discharge from the nose and eyes, coughing, fever, vomiting, seizure, paralysis, diarrhea, and twitching. In the worst cases, it can lead to death. You need to make sure your puppy is vaccinated against this virus at around six weeks of age. Then, your vet will follow up with the vaccines every two to three weeks, until your pup is four months old. A booster shot will be given when your dog turns one.

Canine hepatitis

As a highly contagious virus infection, hepatitis affects the lungs, liver, kidneys, spleen, lungs, and eyes. If infected, your dog will show signs of a fever, vomiting, stomach enlargement, and will feel pain around its liver. The mild forms of the disease can be overcome, but in rare cases, hepatitis can be deadly. Between six and 16 weeks of age, your puppy will receive at least three doses of this vaccine.

Rabies

Rabies is known as a viral disease that harms many mammals and invades their nervous system. This virus causes hallucinations, headaches, anxiety, excessive drooling, paralysis, fear of water, and death. This type of vaccination is mandatory in most states and is taken seriously.

Canine Parvovirus

Unvaccinated puppies that are less than four months of age are at high risk of getting infected with this virus. It attacks the gastrointestinal system, causing fevers, vomiting, and bloody diarrhea.

Non-core vaccinations

Non-core vaccines are optional. Where you live and where you travel with your dog will affect the type of shots it will be taking.

Bordetella bronchiseptica

Leading to the disease known as kennel cough, this bacterium is highly infectious, causing vomiting and severe coughing. In some rare cases, it might cause seizures and death. Injectable vaccines and nasal sprays keep this enemy away.

Canine influenza

Affecting the dog's upper respiratory system, this virus is the canine equivalent for the common flu. It causes nasal discharge, a cough, and sometimes a mild fever. If your dog tends to have more severe symptoms than usual, you may choose to give it this vaccine as a preventative measure.

Bringing home those soft little balls of fur means you're now responsible for your puppy's life. Your dog will depend on you when it comes to your attention, training, and proper veterinary care. It may sound intimidating at first, but by following the right steps, you won't have to worry too much.

Although your dog will need a myriad of check-ups, medications, and vaccinations throughout its life, the frequency of these will mostly depend on its lifestyle. Fortunately, the core preventives will be over early on, and in time, you'll be accustomed to the entire schedule.

Still, your loving little fur baby deserves your undivided attention and care—meaning that you'll have to get used to doing a significant amount of research on canine health. Because it's hard to keep track of these things on your own, make sure you regularly consult a vet for extra help with your puppy's physical health.

I know it seems like a lot, but it is always only in the beginning. Once you get into it, you will find it quite straightforward and with the help of your vet, everything will become much more manageable. So, you have discovered a lot regarding a puppy's health & care in this chapter.

Now you have a complete manual on how to treat your puppy, and you know how to care for it so you, and your puppy can be worry-free. In the next chapter, you will learn what teenage years are, from a dog's perspective and when a dog enters the teenage years. You will also read about how long teenage years last, what to be aware of in this stage of a dog's life, and how to deal with potential problems that your loving companion might present to you.

CHAPTER 6

Dear God, Teenage Years!

What Means Teenage Years In Dog's Perspective

Don't worry, it is not too bad how that might seem. If you have done a great job in puppyhood, you most likely get a really gentle teenage stage of your dog.

So you've survived puppyhood! Housebreaking has been successful, shoes are intact and your puppy is turning into a well-behaved and respectful member of the family. Your job is complete, right? Wrong. Don't get too comfortable yet. Take a deep breath and hold on tight because you are now approaching the teenage years.

We all know the stereotypes surrounding being a teen – moodiness, testing boundaries, resistance to authority, and general rebellion. All are stereotypes because they are, in fact, commonly shared experiences among not only human beings, but most mammals, and that includes dogs!

A dog's teenage years are very similar to a person's, for reasons that are the same: their behaviors are influenced by biological and physiological changes. Dogs in adolescence are coming to terms with the world around them, and forming their sense of self. These years are marked by rebellion, and testing the limits of their parents and authority figures is a prominent theme in adolescent dogs especially.

If you have consistently and patiently trained your puppy, then you have an advantage! Your work now will consist primarily of providing the same guidance and encouragement as before, only now your teen dog will start to rebel. They will want to challenge and question what they've been taught, and they will want to challenge all authority, of course!

Since dogs do not tend to have a multitude of authority figures in their lives, the rebellion is usually aimed at you: the parent and pack leader. However, not all resistance to rules and training is a sign of rebellion alone. Dogs are also questioning everything around them now, and that includes things they already know. Maintain the confidence and patience that you had during your dog's puppyhood, and "answer" your dog's questions with consistent encouragement while continuing to discourage unacceptable behaviors.

When Dog Enters A "Teenage Years"

From the age of six months, your dog enters their "teenage years"! Dogs mature at different rates, and this can vary not only by an individual dog, but also by breed and gender. Among large breeds, a male dog can take a year longer than a female to mature. Maturity doesn't come to your home boxed in a package one day.

Adolescence is a process of reinforcing the rules regarding acceptable behaviors, continuing with consistent positive reinforcement, and helping your dog navigate this highly transitional time. Teenage dogs have an immature brain in an almost-adult body, and their highly instinctive behavior makes understanding the human world around them all the more difficult.

They must come to terms with their limited capabilities not just in the world, but also the limited capabilities of the world around them. Even other dogs will treat them differently: other dogs will hold a now-teen dog accountable for their behaviors, whereas when they were puppies, other dogs tended to cut them some slack. Not anymore! Pushy teenaged dogs will be put in their place by other dogs, and you will see an increase in the occasional fight if you have more than one in your household.

How Long "Teenage Years" Last For

"Teenage years" are not really years. This stage of your dog's life won't last longer than 2 years, usually, it is about 1.5 years. Generally speaking, from the age of six months, until approximately two years, your dog is a teenager! Marking and mounting – colloquially referred to as "humping" - are two behaviors that extend from puppyhood into the teenage years. For dogs that have not been spayed or neutered, these behaviors are much more common.

Hormones

Hormones play a large role in your dog's teen years, as most dogs become sexually mature between 8-12 months of age. Females experience their first estrus (heat) cycle during this time, and males will begin to lift their legs to show interest in dogs of the opposite sex. Dogs mark objects with urine to claim their territory, assert their dominance, and communicate their reproductive status with other dogs.

Having a fully intact reproductive system increases these occurrences, making a dog more apt to mark something to let other dogs know their reproductive status. Males dogs want to let females know that they are available, and females want to attract suitors. Marking is not limited to sexual expression – your dog will participate in urine-marking, regardless or reproductive status, to assert dominance. By urinating on an object, they are claiming their stake, much like a human teenager will do by painting graffiti on a wall or decorating their bedroom. They are expressing themselves!

Sometimes, though, this self-expression appears irrational. Your dog may start marking territory more frequently or aggressively, for seemingly no reason at all. But if you dig down deep enough, you can see that there is a strange sort of logic to their behavior. If, for instance, you notice your dog marking on your shopping bag or backpack, the reason is usually related to the strange scents that your item has picked up during your daily errands. Sometimes the item even has traces of other dogs' markings.

Naturally, this is anathema to a dog who is intent on establishing its own boundaries. Oftentimes you may wonder why a specific chair or table is being marked, only to find that this piece of furniture is near a window that reveals the outside world, where other dogs may be visible to your own dog. The presence of another dog in the neighborhood may not seem like much of an issue to you, but for your dog it is imperative to spread their scent around, just to make sure that the other dog understands which boundaries not to cross.

Marking their territory

From a dog's point of view, these actions are perfectly justified – the dog is simply doing their job and protecting the den. This is why it can sometimes be difficult to deter your dog from this behavior, but doing so is a necessity. Punishing a dog after finding a marking will only confuse them – they won't make the connection between their territorial exploit earlier and your current reprimand. Thus, the best way to solve the problem after discovering a puddle is simply by preventing another one from happening.

First, you must clean up the urine thoroughly, ensuring that not a bit of the scent remains. Dogs often mark the same spot repeatedly, which helps to establish their territory. Sometimes a slapdash soaking up of the urine will leave traces of the scent behind, encouraging your dog to resume its soiling. If the problem area happens to be near a window, close the curtains or otherwise shield your dog from the outside world.

This will reduce their need to reassert their boundaries. If your dog prefers a specific room in which to mark, you can begin to make the room less amenable to soiling. This can be done by feeding your dog in the room as well as giving them treats and other acts of kindness. The room will take on a new meaning and they won't be as inclined to sully it.

So as you can see, there are several reasons for why a dog may mark indoors, and sexual expression is just one of quite a few possible explanations. The same is true for mounting. That may come as a surprise, given the fact that the act itself is essentially as sexually explicit as you can get. But it is indeed more complex than simple "humping."

Things to be aware of

Stay the leader

Dogs in their teen years will start acting up again, just like they did in the beginning of puppyhood. This time it is to challenge the rules that have been put in place to frame their behavior. Destructive behaviors exhibited as a puppy will intensify during the teenage years. Dominance and physical aggression are two ways that dogs challenge their pack leader or parent, even their siblings.

This behavior will pass, but it is imperative that you consistently reinstate boundaries for acceptable behavior in order for it to do so. Digging and chewing are both trademarks of the teenage dog. She's gangly and awkward, and has almost reached their full height. Their legs are longer and their teeth are stronger! Teenage dogs have tremendous amounts of energy that they will channel into destructive behavior if not given enough playtime and exercise.

The destruction that used to be fairly minor will increase exponentially with the size and strength of your dog. Even small dogs will begin to develop much stronger jaws and teeth, making any chewing habits that weren't nipped as a puppy considerably more damaging.

Don't be surprised by the excess of chewing

Chewing in the teen years is often a result of boredom, anxiety, and excess energy in your dog but is also a way to relieve discomfort. Permanent teeth are coming in and your dog needs to chew! A combination of a rebellious nature and the need to chew to comfort their mouths will lead them to chew on anything! In the absence of a toy that satisfies their needs, they will chew on your stuff.

Make sure you continue to provide your teenage dog with interesting and diverse toys to keep them from chewing on the items in your house that do not belong to them. Because larger breeds are now taller, they will have access to places they were unable to get to before, and this should be kept in mind when moving objects out of their reach.

Don't fall for a mouthing

Sometimes your dog will open wide and place its mouth on your hands or arm. They will not bite down, but will just hold their mouth firmly in place, looking at you as if to say, "I'm in charge!" This is called mouthing and is yet another teen behavior used to assert dominance. It can be frightening at first – especially if you have a large teen with a big mouth and big teeth. Rest assured - your dog is not trying to attack you, but instead is trying to take your place as leader. She's challenging you, letting you know that they are bigger and older now and they want to take control.

This is normal. It can happen while playing or simply during petting. Mouthing should be discouraged just like any other unacceptable behavior. Regardless of how natural the act is, putting teeth on human skin is not ok, and if tolerated might lead to aggression. If your dog is inflicting pain or expressing anger when placing its mouth on you, the behavior may be more serious and your dog could be starting to show signs of serious and dangerous aggression.

When you see your dog mounting something or someone, disengage them while firmly and repeatedly saying "No!" Your dog will begin to understand that it is you who is in charge and, however grudgingly, accept their status in the hierarchy. It should be noted, though, that some dogs can be very aggressive and combative when disengaged from mounting.

This is a different set of behavior that must be discouraged, of course, but we must stress that owners of large or powerful dogs should stop trying to disengage a mounting dog if the dog seems especially likely to become violent. The dog's behavior will of course have to be dealt with, but it is not worth risking serious injury at this moment in time. Try to nip mouthing as soon as possible.

Beware of digging

Digging is not only a threat to a well-manicured yard, it is a threat to the safety of your dog. They don't know that, of course, but you do! Deterring your teenage dog from digging means keeping them safe from the harm of getting hit by a car or altercations with other dogs. Your dog knows that they want to explore beyond their boundaries, but they don't know that danger is waiting on the other side.

She may want to go searching for a mate, but does not know that they can encounter highly aggressive dogs and other animals that may have rabies or other diseases that could affect their health – and even the length of their life. If you have a yard, make sure that you continue to supervise your dog during its teenage years. Prevention is often more effective than punishment.

If you notice that your dog has a favorite digging spot – they will probably have several! - deter the act by blocking them from getting to the spot in the first place. Placing stepping stones or bricks over the spot will prevent them from being able to dig. If the area that they like is large, consider placing a small fence or border around the perimeter. Be patient, and know that your dog is not trying to ruin your property or make you angry. They just want to see what the world has to offer!

How To Deal With Potential Problems

Not all unacceptable behaviors during your dog's adolescence are a result of its age. Sometimes your teenage dog will act as if they forgot all that they learned from training as a puppy, and you must continuously revisit various stages of training. Be consistent with reinforcement, but also kind and patient. Your teen dog's attention span is small, and they are easily distracted.

Dear God, Teenage Years!

It might seem as if they are forgetting or ignoring all the work that you've done to teach them to be gentle and well-behaved dogs. Remind them of your place in the pack, and remind them of what is acceptable and what is not. Be patient with your teen – they are experiencing lots of new things and can be easily overwhelmed.

Occasionally bad behavior is indicative of deeper issues. If you notice your dog doing the following, consult your veterinarian or a canine behavioral expert to determine your best course of action:

Soiling the House

Using the bathroom inside of the house should not be confused with urine-marking. Dogs do not want to sleep and eat where they do their business, and continuing to soil the house after puppyhood could be a sign of fear or anxiety, incomplete housebreaking, or a serious medical issue.

Snapping and Biting

Rough play is healthy, normal behavior for a teenage dog. However, when this behavior pushes the boundaries of acceptance and starts looking like mean-spirited aggression, it is cause for concern. If your dog bears their teeth and snarls, they are doubtfully playing anymore, and may be trying to inflict real harm.

Excessive Barking

Barking is, of course, a dog's main form of communication. There is a bevy of things that your dog may be trying to tell you when they bark – they could be alerting you to an intruder, an object or noise that is unfamiliar may have grabbed their attention, or they could just be in a playful mood, trying to get you to join in their games.

Compulsive barking is a different story. Compulsive barkers do so for seemingly no reason at all, and may be motivated simply by boredom. Do not encourage them by yelling while they are barking – this will make them think that you approve of their behavior and are joining in. Instead, try doing something to distract them and positively reinforce their silence.

What Now?

I know you are not a professional dog trainer and probably don't have much experience with dogs either. However, any of the following issues can always be prevented by great parenting in puppyhood. Also, by continuously establishing your alpha position, your dog won't be daring you as much. If your dog respects you greatly, any of these issues won't be such a big deal because by using the power of your position, you will be able to manage your dog's behavior easily and pretty quickly.

Sometimes it will take a little more than playful reinforcement and loving guidance to stop your pushy teenage dog from testing your limits. Remember, always try to lead them towards desired behavior and communicate things with your dog first. These tips are here for you as an addition. So when you feel like popping your teenage dog in the snout, try these tried-and-true hands-free methods of thwarting bad behavior. Use it as a game to your advantage:

Can of Pennies

Take an empty soda can and fill it with enough coins to make it rattle loudly. When your dog is doing something that they should not be doing, like barking incessantly or chewing something that does not belong to them, shake the can. The noise will startle them and interrupt their behavior. Be careful not to shake the can too violently, or put it in your dog's face. This could have the opposite effect, making them nervous, anxious, and fearful.

Compressed Air

Compressed air, like the kind that is used to clean computer keyboards and towers, can be used as an effective tool to interrupt bad behavior. Dogs do not like the sound, and will stop what they are doing to see what is making it. Again, do not chase your dog with the compressed air can, or spray the air at them, or in their face. Your dog will interpret this as an act of aggression or a threat, and react appropriately.

Taste Deterrents

Taste deterrents are substances that are made to taste bad to dogs, in order to deter them from chewing or licking things that they shouldn't. They can be used both indoors and outside, and the bitter taste will repulse your dog, making them associate the taste with the object.

When using a taste deterrent, first apply a small amount to a piece of fabric or paper towel. Place it in your dog's mouth, allowing them to taste it and likely spit it out. If your dog finds the taste unpleasant, they will drool, retch and shake their head. Reapply every 2-4 weeks until your dog is no longer interested in whatever it was they were chewing.

If your dog's bad behavior is still not deterred, you may want to consider professional training classes. Training experts are well-versed in the language of dogs, and are knowledgeable in a wide variety of behavior modification techniques and training exercises that have been proven effective.

Keep on socializing

Socialization is indispensable to an adolescent dog! Exposing your dog to new sights and sounds both lowers their anxiety regarding new things and helps them understand the world around them. Socialization can consist of visits to a dog park, play dates or play groups, and even walks that you already know. Dogs benefit greatly from the company of other dogs and running around with friends is great exercise for your teen dog!

If possible, find a dog park in your area for your family friend to romp around with their own kind for a few hours a week. Sometimes people arrange doggy playdate meet-ups, which are great opportunities for both providing an outlet for energy and exposing your teenage dog to a variety of other dogs and people. Continue to introduce your teenage dog to new, unfamiliar people. Dogs tend to only remain social with ongoing exposure; they are hardwired to be cautious.

Introducing your dogs to new people and exposing them to a variety of social situations will keep their social and behavioral skills up to par. They will be less likely to negatively, or aggressively, respond to unknown guests or visitors. Varying your route when walking your dog will expose them not only to different situations, but also to different terrain. Take them to new neighborhoods, different streets and sidewalks, busy concrete roads, and quiet trails through the woods. These will not only improve their socialization, but they will also stimulate their mind and wear them out!

Teach your dog their own dependency

Teen dogs do not yet have the maturity to be given the run of the house without supervision. They are not yet capable of consistency in thinking and behavior to not let their curiosity take over. Dog-proofing a room is an excellent option when you cannot be supervising your adolescent dog. It is equally important to teach your dog to be alone as it is to socialize with them.

If you never leave your dog alone, it will suffer greatly from separation anxiety when you do. This is not pleasant for your dog – they are literally in a panic because you are not around. They will bark excessively, to the point of causing vomiting and dehydration in extreme cases. they will whine and cry, chew anything they can, usually items that belong to the person they are missing most – you! they will scratch doors and walls in an attempt to escape.

If you have been right by your dog's side since puppyhood, start giving them some space so that they get used to it and are less likely to suffer from separation anxiety. Practice while you are at home: isolate them for short periods of time at first, extending to longer ones as they get more and more comfortable with solitude. Each time, they will show signs of separation anxiety, but these will decrease more and more with time. Reassure them that you are not abandoning them by ending each session with love and affection when you return. The ideal age of starting this process is around 6 months old.

Remember that even though your dog is no longer a puppy, they are still learning. They are going through changes that will temporarily make them stubborn and rebellious, and it will seem as if all previous training and guidance have been forgotten. Do not fault your dog for having a short attention span, questioning its environment, or pushing your limits. This is just the nature of a teenager!

Okay, so now it is time to sit back and enjoy the ride of adolescence! Puppies are very fun and cute, but your teenage dog is ready to begin building a real bond. Adolescent dogs are ready to learn about the world around them, and make distinctions about the people and other dogs in it. You are an important and integral part of your dog's life, continue to be patient and consistent with behavioral training.

And regardless of how frustrated or angry you get, do not hit your dog! Hitting teenage dogs especially is likely to lead to aggression, and that healthy mouthing will turn into unpredictable biting and nipping. This book and the approach discussed in it is all about love. Continue to raise and train your dog with love through their teenage stage and I guarantee you, after that, you will have an incredible, attentive, and loyal companion. All the hustle and training will come to fruition in a way of heartwarming memories.

Conclusion

My lovely friend, we are at the end of this book. I was doing my best to share with you the knowledge I had regarding raising and training a puppy. It was my pleasure to meet with you through the lines of this book.

You have learned so much and I believe you are ready to become an excellent dog parent. In this book, we've covered everything you need to know in order to train and raise your puppy. You have learned basic commands and many tips regarding puppy training. You know how to safely care for the vibrant health of your puppy and you learned the art of positive reinforcement which is the base of dog training.

For the most part, you know how to bond with your puppy and that love is the answer. I hope you find this book very useful, and that it helps you train your dog more effectively. Remember, these are just guidelines and not set-in-stone rules – use all the tips outlined in this book at your discretion. If your dog is showing signs of undesired behavior you are not able to manage, a professional trainer may be able to help.

I promise, the benefits of having a properly trained dog are plentiful and will leave you thrilled with your new-found relationship with man's best friend.

I will now close this book and I wish you the best in your life with your new puppy. So, what are you waiting for? A new, little, cute ball of fur is somewhere waiting for you. I know you have all it takes to be a great dog parent.

I shall meet with you through other pages next time,

With Love,

Sarah

Printed in Great Britain
by Amazon

17401175R00088